Almost Amish is the perfect read if you're feeling the weight of our fancy American lifestyle and looking to simplify your life and get back to the things that matter—like family, home, and community. Nancy paints a wonderful picture of the gift that comes when we slow down and evaluate what's really important and how we can be better stewards of all that God has given us. Not only that, there are practical tips on almost every page about finding ways to emulate an "almost Amish" lifestyle, but the appeal is that they're written in an engaging, informative manner that doesn't make me feel judged because I may still have a weakness for cute shoes and beauty products. Instead, Nancy makes her lifestyle seem so appealing that I'm actually debating putting up a clothesline in my backyard. This is a great book!

MELANIE SHANKLE, A.K.A. BIG MAMA
www.thebigmamablog.com

Almost Amish offers a reminder of the freedom we can uncover through a sustainable lifestyle. Nancy provides real-life examples of ways we can pare down without ditching all technologies. She demonstrates how to emphasize relationships through decisions for how we use our time, money, and other resources. Her personal choices remind us of the joy we can recapture when we prioritize strategies for simple living.

SARAH PULLIAM BAILEY
Christianity Today

Tyndale House Publishers, Inc.
Carol Stream, Illinois

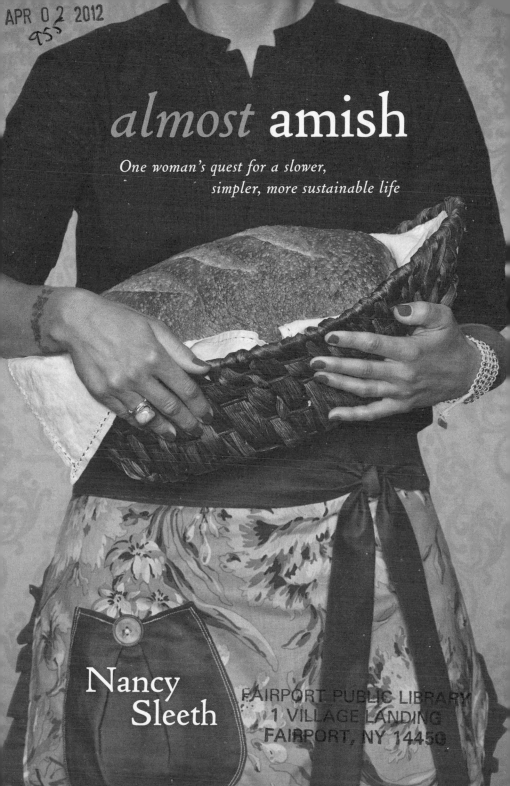

almost amish

One woman's quest for a slower,
simpler, more sustainable life

Nancy
Sleeth

Visit Tyndale online at www.tyndale.com.

Visit the author's online site, www.blessedearth.org.

TYNDALE and Tyndale's quill logo are registered trademarks of Tyndale House Publishers, Inc.

Published in association with the literary agency of Daniel Literary Group, Nashville, Tennessee.

Library of Congress Cataloging-in-Publication Data

Sleeth, Nancy.
  Almost Amish : one woman's quest for a slower, simpler, more sustainable life / Nancy Sleeth.
    p. cm.
  ISBN 978-1-4143-2699-3 (sc)
  1. Conduct of life. 2. Amish—Conduct of life. I. Title.
  BJ1589.S544 2012
  248.4—dc23   2011049845

Printed in the United States of America

18	17	16	15	14	13	12
7	6	5	4	3	2	1

Contents

Introduction *ix*

1. Homes *1*
   *Homes are simple, uncluttered, and clean;
   the outside reflects the inside.*

2. Technology *21*
   *Technology serves as a tool and does not rule
   as a master.*

3. Finances *47*
   *Saving more and spending less bring
   financial peace.*

4. Nature *71*
   *Time spent in God's creation reveals
   the face of God.*

5. Simplicity *93*
   Small and local leads to saner lives.

6. Service *109*
   *Service to others reduces loneliness
   and isolation.*

7. Security *129*
   The only true security comes from God.

8. Community *149*
   *Knowing neighbors and supporting local
   businesses build community.*

9. Families *171*
   Family ties are lifelong; they change but never cease.
10. Faith *195*
    Faith life and way of life are inseparable.

Almost Amish Recipes *217*
Additional Resources *233*
Questions for Discussion *235*
Acknowledgments *241*
About the Author *245*

Introduction

Going back can sometimes be the quickest way forward.
C. S. LEWIS, *Mere Christianity*

"WHAT ARE YOU, Amish or something?" a large man with a booming voice asked from the back of the room. I was not surprised by the question, but the tone rattled me a bit.

Open your eyes! I wanted to reply. *Am I wearing a bonnet? We arrived in a Prius, not on a pony.*

The question came at the close of a long day, at the end of a demanding speaking tour. I was tired, but that's no excuse for my less-than-gracious thoughts. It was not the first time my family had been compared to the Amish, nor would it be the last. So why did this question stay with me, long after the seminar ended?

Over the previous few years my husband, Matthew, and I had gone around the country giving nearly a thousand talks, sermons, workshops, and retreats about the scriptural call to care for God's creation. We wrote books on the subject. We made films. From Washington state to Washington, DC, we had fielded questions on everything from lightbulbs to the light of Jesus, from water bottles to living waters, from soil erosion to the four kinds of soils. The Q&A session was usually our favorite part of the seminar.

As a teacher, I often said that there are no bad questions. This one, as it turns out, was especially good because it forced me to examine my life in new ways and increased my appreciation for many of the choices my family has made. Now, a few years later, I feel nothing but gratitude for this man's question, as it marked the beginning of a fulfilling journey. But before I share our Almost Amish story, I have to backtrack a bit.

How We Got Here

Just a decade ago, my husband had been at the peak of his career—director of emergency services and chief of medical staff at a hospital. He loved taking care of patients, and I loved caring for our two children, Clark and Emma. We lived in a postcard-perfect New England town, in a beautiful home filled with beautiful things. Our kids sailed in the summer and skied in the winter, carefully dressed to L. L. Bean perfection. In the spirit of laid-back luxury, dinner parties featured lobster caught a block from our home. "Trustafundians," as Matthew called our wealthiest neighbors, moored their wooden sailboats at the village yacht club. We were living out the American dream, enjoying the affluence and status of a successful physician's family.

But bad stuff began to happen to us, as it does to everyone. Matthew and I had been raised in different faith traditions, and when we got married, our families weren't happy about it. So we said, "If that's what religion is about, forget it!" For two decades we drifted along until three crises hit, one after another.

During a family reunion, my brother died in a drowning accident in front of our kids. I was devastated, depressed, disoriented. Not long afterward, a mentally ill patient who had been in the ER began stalking Matthew. The patient's behavior, culminating with his conviction of a vile murder, put a strain on our family. Then, during the course of one week, Matthew admitted three different women to the hospital—all in their thirties, all with breast cancer, all destined to die.

This last experience was more subtle, but no less disturbing. One woman had seizures for about forty-five minutes in the ER, and Matthew could not stabilize her. He had to go out to the waiting room and tell the husband, who had two young kids, that his wife was gone. Matthew then did what any compassionate doctor would do: he hugged the young dad, and they cried together.

That night, Matthew came home upset. His own wife (me!) was just a few years older than the woman who died. "What are the odds?" he asked. So we looked in his textbook from medical school, which said that one in nineteen women had a lifetime chance of getting breast cancer. The updated version of that same textbook said one in nine women, and the odds have gotten even worse since then. Matthew asked if it was time not only to be "running for the cure," as it said on the back of our cereal boxes, but to begin looking for the cause.

Around this time, we went on a family vacation to a barrier

island off the coast of Florida. After playing in the ocean all day, the kids went to bed early, and that night Matthew and I relaxed on the balcony, enjoying a peaceful breeze beneath silent stars. So rarely did we have time to stop and think, to discuss the big questions of life. Our conversation rambled from the kids to work to books to global concerns.

That's when I asked Matthew two questions that would change our lives forever. First question: "What is the biggest problem facing the world today?"

His answer: "The world is dying." And he wasn't just talking about his patients. There are no elms left on Elm Street, no cod at Cape Cod. "If we don't have a stage where we can play out the other issues, things like war and poverty and AIDS won't really matter."

Question number two was more difficult: "If the world is dying, what are we going to do about it?"

Matthew didn't have an immediate answer. But he said he'd get back to me. And after vacation, we both set out to find an answer.

Together we embarked on a faith and environmental journey. We read many of the world's great sacred texts, finding much wisdom but not the answers we were seeking. Then one slow night in the ER, Matthew picked up an orange book. It was a Bible. We didn't have one at home, so he stole it.

No worries: it was a Gideon Bible. And as the Gideons would have hoped, Matthew read the Gospels and ran smack dab into a remarkable figure: Jesus. Suddenly my husband found the Truth he had been seeking.

One by one, our entire family followed. And that changed everything—the books we read, the music we listened to, the people we hung out with, and most of all how we learned to love God and love our neighbors by caring for his creation.

Eventually, Matthew got back to me about my second question. His answer: he would quit his job as a physician and spend the rest of his life trying to serve God and save the planet, even if he never earned another cent.

Hmmm. A job without a description. Or salary. Or benefits.

My response: "Honey, are you sure we need to do that much about it?"

Shock was quickly followed by panic. And fear. We had two preteen kids, and college was just around the corner. How would we put food on the table, let alone pay for those Ivy League educations the kids were both on the fast track toward?

Feelings are a moving target, but the Bible remains stead-fast. Tony Campolo once wrote that the words *fear not* are repeated 365 times in the Bible—one reassurance for each day of the year. The devil wants us to worry, but God wants us to trust in him. Philippians 4:6 tells us to cast all our worries upon Jesus and be anxious for nothing.

Easier said than done. I was staggered by the implications of my husband's answer, but that terror was soon replaced by a desire to learn more. So we began studying what Scripture had to say about living more simply. We read through the entire Bible, underlining everything that had to do with caring for God's creation.

Matthew 7 seemed to speak directly to our family: "Why

worry about a speck in your friend's eye when you have a log in your own? . . . Hypocrite! First get rid of the log in your own eye; then you will see well enough to deal with the speck in your friend's eye."

We took Jesus' advice and began cleaning up our own act before worrying about cleaning up the rest of the world. The transition—as much emotional and spiritual as physical—took a couple of years. One of the very first things we did was to take an accounting—a measure of our ecological footprint. We had always thought of ourselves as environmentally aware—using cloth diapers, stocking up on reusable shopping bags, and recycling. But when we actually calculated our total use of resources, we found ourselves exactly average for Americans. Not bad for a physician's family—since in general the more income people have, the more resources they consume—but still, we were clearly using more than our fair share on a global scale: about *six times* more energy than our neighbors around the world.

So we began to scale back. At first the steps were small: adjust the thermostat a few degrees. Clean out some closets. Start a vegetable garden. These small changes led to bigger ones: shop for clothes at consignment stores. Plant some fruit trees and berry bushes. Eat local foods in season. The more we did, the more we wanted to do. Before long, we found ourselves ditching the TV and replacing the family sedan with a hybrid car.

Changes in one area of our life led to changes in other areas. At home, we installed water-saving showerheads, got rid of the clothes dryer, and replaced the refrigerator with a smaller, superefficient model. Outside, we avoided chemicals, planted shade trees, and stopped mowing the backyard.

Transitioning back to classroom teaching, I began biking to work and setting up bins for paper recycling. Based on student energy audits of the buildings, we made recommendations for cutting back on electricity costs—switching to LED bulbs in exit signs and installing automatic light detectors. The school switched to double-sided printing, cutting paper use in the library by 50 percent.

We gave away one of our cars to a church family with no transportation, substituting human power and carpooling to get where we needed to go. Our food intake became less processed and more real, less meat-based and more healthful. The vegetable garden doubled in size, and we began canning and preserving food year round.

With everyone in our family on the same page, we had a new standard against which to measure ourselves—not our next-door neighbors, who produced four bags of trash to our one—but Jesus, who did not have a place to lay his head at night and beseeched the rich man to sell everything and give it to the poor.

Little changes added up. Eventually, we got rid of half our possessions and moved to a house with the same footprint of our old garage. (As Matthew likes to say, "Don't feel too sorry for us—it was a doctor's sized garage!") In the process, we eventually reduced our energy consumption by more than two-thirds and our trash production by nine-tenths.

But it was more than just an ecological movement: the changes toward simplicity that we made on the outside started to change us on the inside. As my grandmother used to say, "Act kind, and then you become kind." Sabbath, the principle of rest God imparted to the Hebrews, became the high point of our week. Preparation began on Saturday, with the kids finishing their homework and everyone pitching in to clean the house. To our delight, Clark and Emma became the biggest defenders of our weekly day of rest. The Hebrew word for "holy" is *kadosh,* which means "set apart." Sunday became a holy day, set apart for God, for family, and for renewal. It was what we lived for.

These changes altered the lens through which we viewed not only the "holy day" of Sunday but all the holidays. Instead of cartloads of Christmas presents and garbage bags of wrapping paper, we limited gifts to small stocking treats and gave the rest of the money we would have spent to a family in need. Knocking on a door and anonymously leaving a bundle of babysitting savings became a favorite holiday tradition.

These material changes also affected how we spent our time. With no TV, we read and talked and listened to music together more. Instead of playing computer games, we went for walks outdoors. An hour spent in nature became an hour studying the face of God.

School remained important, but for new reasons. Emma started a morning Bible study group. Baking all the snacks for a by-teens, for-teens student worship service became a central fixture of her week. Clark began talking about a full-time calling in missionary medicine and looking into Christian colleges. Relationships, rather than résumé building, became both the means and the end.

The changes we were making in ourselves rippled outward in concentric circles—first in our family, then in our church, then throughout our community. We led streambed cleanups, tree-planting efforts, and discussions on faith and the environment. People began to grow curious about this evangelical Christian family who "hugged trees," and a man-who-bit-the-dog fascination with our story widened.

After we had our own house in order, we felt called to share our journey. Matthew wrote a book called *Serve God, Save the Planet: A Christian Call to Action.* Using stories from our family's life and his experience working in the ER, he explained the theological and medical reasons why our family made these changes, inspiring others to do the same.

People liked the book—a lot. It's an easy book to read, but hard to ignore. We received letters from readers who felt called to change but didn't know where to start. So I wrote *Go Green, Save Green*—sharing stories about what worked, what didn't, and what our family learned in the process. To handle all the speaking and workshop requests, we started a nonprofit organization, Blessed Earth, and thus a ministry was born.

And that's how a just-about-Jewish girl found herself in a Bible-Belt church being asked by a man with a booming voice if she were Amish. Despite abundant physical evidence to the contrary, I can see where the question came from. We had just answered a series of questions about laundry.

"Is it true that you hang your clothes on a clothesline?" *Yes, we do—outside in summer and in the basement in winter.*

"Does hanging your clothes really make a difference?" *Each load saves five pounds of harmful gases from being emitted, so this is a tangible way I can show my love for our global neighbors and my respect for God's creation.*

"Will doing that save me money?" *Nearly a hundred bucks a year: the clothes dryer consumes more electricity than any appliance in your home except the refrigerator. Plus your clothes will smell fresher and last longer—that lint in the dryer is made up of cloth fibers.*

"Doesn't it take more time?" *Yes, and that's what I love about it. It gives me a break from working at the computer, and I get to pray or listen to birds or talk with my husband and kids as they work beside me. Best of all, hanging up clothes gives me a chance to hang out with God.*

So the question about whether I was Amish seemed glib to me—until I realized its significance. Most people equate drying clothes on a line with poverty—it's what people do in poorer countries or in the most economically depressed neighborhoods in the United States. To air dry clothes by choice is countercultural. And who, more than any other group in twenty-first-century America, is both countercultural and committed to air drying clothes? Has intact families? Healthy communities? Gardens, home-cooked meals, and uncluttered homes? Restrained use of technology, strong local economies, and almost nonexistent debt?

Most of all, what group has kept simplicity, service, and

faith at the center of all they say and do? The Amish! All of which led to my epiphany: *few of us can become Amish, but all of us can become almost Amish.*

Of course I wasn't Amish, but I guess I had become something approaching it. Could other people do the same? It was time for me to start exploring what an Almost Amish life would really look like.

A Brief History of the Amish

The Amish are a Christian denomination that began in the Protestant Reformation of sixteenth-century Europe. Their religious ancestors were called *Anabaptists* (rebaptizers) because the first converts were adults who already had been baptized as babies.

A group of Swiss Anabaptists began to study the Gospels earnestly. They were especially moved by Christ's teachings on love and nonresistance and felt called to imitate his life and character. Christ was present not only in the sacraments but in the body of believers who practiced his teachings. While this may seem like mainstream teaching to us now, it was considered dangerous theology at the time.

The Swiss Anabaptists proposed a set of reforms. The state-run church responded by burning, drowning, starving, or decapitating about twenty-five hundred Anabaptist leaders. Understandably, the remaining Anabaptists went underground or fled to rural enclaves.

In the late 1600s, Jakob Ammann emerged as an Anabaptist

leader. Ammann's followers, eventually known as the Amish, became a separate group within the Anabaptists. To an outsider, Ammann's differences with the parent church seem little more than a family quarrel over foot washing, grooming styles, and the extent of "shunning"—social avoidance of those who had been excommunicated.

In the early 1700s, the Amish began to seek fertile farmland in the New World and eventually established communities in Pennsylvania, the Midwest, and several Canadian provinces. The Amish and their Anabaptist cousins, the Mennonites, often settled in neighboring communities.

Starting in the twentieth century, the Amish population has doubled every twenty years—due to birthrates, not evangelism—with the total population in 2010 standing at around a quarter million.

Principles to Live By

The Amish are by no means a perfect people. Their example, however, does have much to teach us. How can we incorporate the best of Amish principles into our modern lives? To answer this, I did some reading. And some visiting. And some listening. I in no way pretend to be an expert on the Amish, but the more I read and visited and listened, the more I found to admire. The Amish are islands of sanity in a whirlpool of change.

Along the way, I discovered some Amish principles that we can *all* try to emulate. These principles (similar to the list that Wendell Berry laid out more than two decades ago in *Home Economics*) provide guidelines for a simpler, slower, more sustainable life. They offer me hope.

1. Homes are simple, uncluttered, and clean; the outside reflects the inside.
2. Technology serves as a tool and does not rule as a master.
3. Saving more and spending less bring financial peace.
4. Time spent in God's creation reveals the face of God.
5. Small and local leads to saner lives.
6. Service to others reduces loneliness and isolation.
7. The only true security comes from God.
8. Knowing neighbors and supporting local businesses build community.
9. Family ties are lifelong; they change but never cease.
10. Faith life and way of life are inseparable.

Throughout the following pages, I will be sharing stories from the wide range of Anabaptist traditions, including Amish, Mennonite, Hutterite, and Brethren. Just as there are widely divergent practices among those who call themselves "Methodist" or "Baptist," these Anabaptist communities differ one from another. Even within the Amish, there are subdivisions ranging from those who worship in homes and would shun any member who drove a car (Old Order Amish) to those who meet in churches and allow ownership of motorized vehicles (Beachy Amish, the followers of Moses Beachy). What they all share are a respect for tradition, a desire to make conscious decisions about "progress," and a belief that Scripture should guide every action—not just for a few hours on Sunday, but in our homes and throughout the week.

The home is the threshold of the Almost Amish life; come join me on the front porch, and together we will begin our journey.

CHAPTER I

HOMES

Homes are simple, uncluttered, and clean;
the outside reflects the inside.

LAST SUMMER, our daughter interned with a publishing company. Emma's mentor assigned her a wide range of challenging projects, and she learned a lot from them all. But the assignment where she felt as though she had the most editing input was an Amish romance novel.

Dubbed "bonnet books" or Amish love stories (my husband jokingly calls them "bonnet rippers"), these G-rated romances usually center on an Amish person who falls for an outsider. Most of the authors are women, such as Beverly Lewis, who has sold fourteen million copies of her novels, set among the Amish in Pennsylvania. In recent years, the genre has expanded to include Amish thrillers and murder mysteries.

And then there is the 1985 movie *Witness*, where millions formed lasting impressions of the Amish. *Witness* is the story

1

of a young Amish boy who sees someone murdered in a train station. A police officer goes into hiding in Amish country to protect him and is attracted to the boy's beguiling mother. A trifecta of thriller, mystery, and romance, the film grossed sixty-five million dollars and won a dozen awards.

Why the popularity of Amish-themed books and movies? Publishers attribute their success to pastoral settings and forbidden love. No doubt, the Romeo-and-Juliet winning formula is partly responsible. But rogue romance cannot explain why each year eleven thousand motor coaches and more than eleven million tourists visit Lancaster County, Pennsylvania—the epicenter of Amish country.

While our fascination with Amish culture is complex, one facet is clear: people are drawn to the simplicity of the Amish home. The Amish home is a symbol of something missing in our plugged-in, nanosecond-paced lives. It is difficult to see something that has disappeared. Our image of the white Amish farmhouse fills a void that we cannot even describe. It reminds us of what we have lost.

Home as Haven

Jesus says that the inside of us should be as clean as the outside (see Matthew 23:25). Amish families apply this principle to every area of life, including their physical surroundings. The Amish farmhouse, inside and out, is clean, uncluttered, and unpretentious. Their homes reflect their values: careful management, simplicity, and orderliness.

If you drive around Lancaster County in the summer, you will see farm after farm with everything in its place. No rusting cars up on cinder blocks. No falling down barns. No trash heaps. Gardens are filled with orderly rows of vegetables and colorful flowers—all to the glory of God.

Amish homes are beautiful in their simplicity. Families purchase things, but only things they need. They do not call attention to themselves with flashy technology, decorating, or clothes. That would be considered prideful, and Scripture is full of warnings about where pride can lead.

The Amish do not believe that the material world is bad. Rather, they believe that beautiful things that last many generations are part of God's creation and should be treasured. To loosely paraphrase Keats, beautiful craftsmanship is "a joy forever."

Family ties are strengthened by the architecture of their homes. The physical structure of the Amish home is designed to accommodate multiple generations living together. Grandparents live in an apartment within the home or in a *Grossdawdy Haus*, a small adjacent house. The home is a haven for all generations, where wisdom is respected and each person plays an important role. Dependence upon one another is seen not as a weakness but as a strength.

Building an Almost Amish Life

One physical trait my husband shares with Amish men is an oversize right forearm. Those muscles come from years of swinging a hammer in the days before (noisy!) nail guns.

I met Matthew when I was home studying for my first set of college finals. A really good-looking guy had come to install a bay window in the kitchen. As Matthew likes to say, my parents' worst nightmare began to unfold before their eyes: their eighteen-year-old daughter fell in love with the carpenter.

When we married, I told Matthew that he was the smartest person I had ever met and that maybe he should think about going to college. Three years of undergrad school, four years of medical school, and three years of residency later, Matthew embarked on his ER career and built us a beautiful home on the coast of Maine.

Though fancier than an Amish home, it had the same emphasis on craftsmanship and simplicity. Built in the classic Greek Revival style, it was designed to last for centuries: oak floors, cherry cabinetry, maple butcher-block counters, solid-wood doors, uncompromising structural integrity, and a Rumford fireplace to keep us warm on winter nights.

Had we lived in an Amish community, much of our artwork and furnishings would have seemed ostentatious. And certainly the electric lines that powered our appliances would have been taboo. The house itself would not have seemed too big *if* it had been filled with seven or eight children, several grandchildren, and a couple of grandparents. But with only four inhabitants, our home seemed unjustifiably large. After our spiritual and environmental conversion experience, we knew we needed to downsize. And with Matthew's leaving medicine for a calling that had no job title and no salary, it made sense to sell the big house and bank the savings.

So we moved, and when Matthew left medicine, his carpentry skills came in very handy. He designed a much smaller home, also based on the Greek Revival farmhouse tradition, only this time more consciously in keeping with passive-solar building design and with many energy-saving features built in. Because of careful positioning, the house essentially warmed itself in winter and shut off the sun's rays in summer. Instead of our previous Rumford fireplace, already more efficient than most, we included a superefficient Russian counterflow woodstove: six thousand pounds of soapstone and heat-sink masonry, which gave off a steady heat throughout the day. If we built one fire in the morning, the stove emitted heat until nightfall.

We lived in that home while the kids were in high school. Both received scholarships to Asbury University in Lexington—Clark first, and Emma a year later. Because Emma was fifteen when she was accepted, we followed our kids to college. Neither had a driver's license yet, so—strange but true—our children asked us to move nearby.

Not long ago, we moved yet again, this time to a town house in Kentucky. Our children have now graduated from college, and we all live in the same neighborhood—Emma with her college roommate and Clark with his bride, Valerie. Our house is only eighteen feet wide, so it's easier to clean and care for. We had to give up some things, such as a yard, but I found a community garden where I continue to grow vegetables and work the earth. No big house or yard care means more time for family, friends, and God. We are entering a new stage of life, and our house reflects our changing needs and values.

Jesus says we are supposed to be ready to leave everything to follow him. In our family's case, we have, but with a cost. We feel it. Our children feel it. Though our home is peaceful, uncluttered, and calming, we lack the permanence and history of an Amish home. I hope that Lexington will be our last home, for my heart yearns to put down roots and stay.

A home, after all, is more than four walls: it is shelter against the tempests of life, a place to welcome friends, and a nest—after our travels—to which we long to return.

The Almost Amish Way: Keep the Home Uncluttered

So what is the Almost Amish way? While no single action will guarantee that you will have a calm, peaceful, uncluttered home, these suggestions can help you along the journey:

Keep stuff out

When we moved to the town house, we saw it as another chance to donate things we no longer needed to the local refugee ministry. But getting rid of stuff is a short-term solution; keeping things out of the house in the first place is the cure.

One tactic is to avoid temptations. To this end, Matthew and I receive very few catalogs in the mail. This does not happen by accident. Every year or so, I visit the Direct Marketing Association website (www.dmachoice.org) and Catalog Choice (www.catalogchoice.org) to take our names off any mailing lists that we no longer want to be on. It takes only a few minutes, and it greatly reduces the stream of junk mail we receive. I also save up any catalogs that make it to our mailbox and call the 800 number to ask to be removed from their mailing lists.

But there is an exception: the Lehman's Non-Electric Catalog, with the most retro collection of useful items I've ever seen. We've been on this mailing list for close to three decades. Founded in 1955 to serve the local Amish and others without electricity, this store carries old-fashioned, high-quality merchandise that is difficult to find anywhere else. "My idea was to preserve the past for future generations," says owner Jay Lehman. "I was concerned that some day the Amish would not be able to maintain their simple ways of life because these products would no longer be available." His goal was, and still is, to provide authentic products for those seeking a simpler life.

Does Lehman's carry stuff I don't need? Of course. But it also carries useful tools and home items that last, well, at least a lifetime. It is where we purchased our oil lamps two decades ago and where we have ordered our replacement mantles and wicks. It's where you can find all kinds of products you thought they quit making years ago: apple peelers, potato ricers, and butter churns for the kitchen; straight razors, shaving brushes, and soap-making supplies for the bath; and heavy-duty suspenders, straw hats, and walking sticks for the Almost Amish fashion statement.

I practically do cartwheels when this catalog arrives. Matthew and I vie for first dibs. He tends to dog-ear the "manly" pages—offering wood-carrying implements, hand tools, and pocketknives—as well as those featuring anything with "LED," "solar," or "rechargeable" in its title. For my part, everything in the kitchen section (except the butchering supplies) cries out to me; it requires Amish-like self-control not to order things I can borrow from neighbors or continue to live without. *But those red gingham reusable sandwich pouches look so cute and eco-friendly. . . .*

While the catalog is full of things that make sense and I would like to own, the Amish way is to buy only things that are truly needed. I'm not surprised that Lehman's now sells more to non-Amish folks than to the Amish. The Amish keep their homes uncluttered by *not* buying things they will use only a few times or Grandpa already owns or the kids will play with once and then lose in their overstuffed closets.

Invest in quality

The things that Matthew and I have in our home are mostly handmade, high quality, and durable—items we can pass along to our children and to their children. Even when we were poor newlyweds, we invested in quality. One example is the hutch we have in our dining room.

When Matthew and I were first married, I worked as a

technical writer; on my lunch break, I sometimes stopped by an antique store. It was there that I saw a chestnut hutch with Amish-like carvings and a warm patina that comes only from generations of use. Matthew, though deeply engrossed in his pre-med studies, also happened to pass by the same antique store where, among hundreds of items, he was most drawn to the chestnut hutch, too.

A month or two passed. Neither of us said anything to the other. But then one Saturday we walked into the store together. The store owner must have been chuckling under his breath: both of us had stopped in many times separately to admire the hutch. Now here we were together. The secret was revealed.

Although Matthew and I are both conservative when it comes to spending, in the glow of youth we did something very uncharacteristic: we decided to trade in much of our furniture—an oak Empire sideboard and three wobbly wooden chairs—plus most of our small cash reserves for the hutch. In an act of charity, the store owner accepted our offer. We carefully transported our purchase to the apartment—a four-hundred-square-foot, second-floor flat—and filled the hutch with the china my grandmother had given us for our wedding present.

It was one of the best investments we ever made. There is no way we could afford that hutch today. It is as stunning as it was thirty years ago—more valuable, more cherished, and more beautiful than the day we purchased it. And I have little doubt that it will be passed along to our children and to our children's children.

The Amish understand that longevity is a form of sustainability. In the end, things that do not have to be replaced require fewer resources and cause less wear and tear on the bank account and on the earth that God created to sustain us all.

Make the kitchen the heart of your home

A kitchen does not have to be fancy to make it the center of family life. Though their kitchens lack granite countertops, stainless steel appliances, and twenty-five-cubic-foot electric refrigerators, the Amish spend far more time and produce many times more food in their kitchens than do most other Americans. Not only do they lack electric refrigerators—they lack electric anything. Think about it: no stand mixer, no food processor, no blender, no slow cooker, no popcorn popper, no toaster oven, no microwave.

Remember all the must-have appliances in days gone by? In the 1970s, the electric can opener, the electric knife, and the electric trash compactor were standard-issue equipment. Thumb through a kitchenware catalog and you'll see many other must-have items that will seem equally expendable a decade from now.

The kitchen in our town house is smaller than any I have had since our pre-kid days. Yet I produce more meals from this kitchen than at any time in my life. During a typical week, we host several gatherings with friends, neighbors, and colleagues—ranging from three people to twenty or more. In addition, Friday night is family night, when our children often also invite their friends to our table.

Matthew appreciates good food, and I like to prepare it, but with so many guests, I have learned to keep things simple. Soup, salad, and homemade bread are my standard offerings. I rely on excellent, no-fail recipes for mushroom, creamy potato, and curried lentil soups. (See the appendix for tried-and-true recipes.) As the seasons permit, I branch out into cream of asparagus, broccoli, and vegetable-whatever soup. Whenever we go out to eat on our travels, I check out new soups and try to re-create them at home. Right now, I'm working on a spicy ginger pumpkin recipe.

One of the many exceptions that make my lifestyle *almost* Amish is my technique for bread making. I mix the dough and complete the first rising in a bread maker (forty-five minutes on my quick-rise setting) and then shape the dough, do the second rising, and bake the bread in the traditional manner. You have not tasted heaven until you've had my braided challah—the traditional Jewish egg bread served on Friday nights.

Salads are creative opportunities. In my vegetable garden, I grow a wide range of colorful greens from spring to fall. The garden provides tomatoes in various shapes and colors, along with many other vegetables as equal-opportunity salad enhancers. In winter, I rely on dried cranberries, sharp cheeses, nuts, and homemade croutons to give substance to the salad. For a simple dinner, I might add grilled chicken or salmon as an optional topping. Always, I make my own vinaigrette.

The Bible is explicit about the importance of hospitality. Think about Abraham entertaining the angels under the oaks of Mamre, Rebekah watering Eliezer's ten camels at the well, Lazarus opening his home to Jesus and his motley crew, Zacchaeus being stunned and humbled to have Jesus over for supper—these are examples of people who shared their table with others. Paul also explicitly states that willingness to offer hospitality is a qualification for becoming a church elder (see 1 Timothy 3:2). As my husband likes to say, no one knows whether the fish that fed five thousand were broiled, baked, or fried; what we do know is that the spirit of generosity and the miracle of faith ensured that there was plenty for all.

Most of us are familiar with the parable of the wedding banquet told in Matthew 22:1-14. A king invites guests to a great feast. But when the time comes, most of the guests who sent in a positive RSVP find themselves too busy with business meetings or piano recitals or the big game on TV to show up. Jesus is making the point that God has prepared a feast for each of us—eternal life—yet many of us get too consumed with the busyness of existence to accept his grace-filled invitation.

It is no accident that Jesus uses a meal to illustrate his point. The parable is not only about eternal life but also about life here on earth. And it is not just about how to be a good guest but how to become a welcoming host. Three times a day, twenty-one times a week, we are given opportunities to act like the King. We are to invite all to our table, not only family and those who can reciprocate, but especially the single mother, the exchange student, or the disabled person in our pews.

As hymnist Charles Gabriel wrote in 1895,

"All things are ready," come to the feast!
Come, for the table now is spread;
Ye famishing, ye weary, come,
And thou shalt be richly fed.

It is not the number of fancy gadgets or beautiful serving platters that matters; rather it's the hands that prepare the meals and the holy communion that takes place when we share our table with others that make our kitchens the heart of the home.

Clean out your bedroom closets

The Amish wear plain clothes—homemade dresses and aprons for women and simple pants and shirts for men. They eschew patterned fabric and even buttons, which could be considered ostentatious, and instead rely upon hook-and-eye closures and suspenders. Women cover their heads and dress modestly. They avoid using appearance as a form of self-expression or to attract attention to their bodies, which can lead to pride.

I do not dress as plainly as the Amish: many of my clothes have buttons, I wear some patterned fabrics, and I cover my head only when it gets cold outside. But my closet, nonetheless, reflects my values, as it does for each of us.

I tend to wear long dresses and gravitate toward looser-fitting clothes, for comfort as much as modesty. Almost all my clothes are secondhand. The reason: I cannot justify the huge amount of water, fossil fuels, and chemicals that go into manufacturing, shipping, displaying, and advertising the clothes that fill our malls. Killing the planet so I can look fashionable just does not seem like a good trade-off.

I wish I could sew. My son's mother-in-law is a math genius but also a fabulous seamstress. She sewed all the dresses for Valerie and Clark's wedding. But if I cannot sew, I can at least mimic some of the values the Amish demonstrate in their closets.

First, keep it simple. Despite what the magazines tell you, only those with darker coloring look good in orange—period.

Second, don't try to keep up with the latest fashions. Designers spend billions to convince us that brown is the new black and the tie width we thought respectable three years ago is now totally out.

Third, avoid malls. "Lead us not into temptation, but deliver us from evil." Emma was twelve before she ever went to a mall, and then only went because her adopted big sister/ favorite babysitter Kate felt sorry for her and took her on her birthday. When they returned home, Kate said she wasn't sure if Emma had a good time—she seemed a little overwhelmed.

Well, I consider that a sign of good health. I am more than a little overwhelmed myself—every year or two—when I step into a mall. I leave feeling fat, ugly, and decidedly uncool. Of course, that is what department stores are designed to do, so they can sell us on the lie that buying their products will make us as thin, gorgeous, and hip as the ten-foot models in their displays. "Fancy Nancy" is just as oxymoronic as "Fashionable Amish."

Fourth, clean out your clothes closets. Matthew is ruthless when it comes to his closet—if he has not worn something in the past year, it gets donated to Goodwill or the Salvation Army. When we go on the road, he wears outfit A (a gray suit) or outfit B (khaki pants, white shirt, and navy sports coat). Pretty much the rest of the time, it's outfit B minus the sports coat, though occasionally he gets wild and wears the blue oxford shirt instead of the white. The end result is that clothes take up very little room in his closet . . . or his thoughts.

Few of us today have the talent or skill to sew our own clothes. Yet even so, the Amish probably spend considerably fewer total hours on their wardrobes than the average sixteen-year-old in America. Reading fashion magazines, staying up with the dos and don'ts, driving to the mall, returning clothes that don't fit, and shopping on the Internet sap our time and energy. As one of my favorite poets, William Wordsworth, said more than a century ago, "Getting and spending, we lay waste our powers."

And that's what the fashion industry is to the Amish—not

only a waste, but a distraction from the family, friends, and faith that really (should) matter.

Clean out your vanity

The average American family spends fifty-five to eighty-five dollars per month on toiletries. I would be surprised if our family spent eighty-five dollars a year, even though I try to buy natural and organic products, which tend to cost more per ounce. The reason is that I just don't buy most of the products big business tries to convince me I need to stay clean, beautiful, and young. That means no hair dyes. No special anti-aging creams (okay, almost none). All my makeup fits in one small pencil case. My blow dryer is a vintage 1970s model—the Vidal Sassoon my mom bought back when the Dorothy Hamill bob became the rage. It's large and awkward and shaped like a dangerous weapon, but, hey—if it ain't broke, why replace it?

Of course the Amish would not even own a hair dryer, and they don't wear any makeup at all. But my husband thinks they (and Hasidic Jews, who dress rather similarly) are the prettiest women around. I agree. One of the most charming—and rare—qualities is being beautiful without knowing it.

Think of the most attractive older woman you know. Besides my mom, whom I love above all else, the woman who comes to my mind has gray hair, worn just above her shoulders. The only cosmetic I ever recall seeing her wear is clear lip balm. Her eyebrows are thick and expressive. She's in great shape, her body strong and her movements spritely. But the traits I notice first are her smile and her prolonged hug. Though blessed with six children and a dozen grandchildren of her own, every time I enter her home she treats me like a daughter she has been waiting to see. The lines around her mouth and eyes deepen when she laughs with me, and she continues to hold my hand while we talk. She is one of the most lovely women I know.

We've seen photos of people in the public eye who, because of a fear of aging and constant scrutiny by the press, end up with distorted bodies and unexpressive faces. Too much attention to their naturally lovely features ultimately makes them less, rather than more, attractive. While most of us are not celebrities, each of us should be wary of focusing too much of our time on appearances. For physical and for spiritual reasons, we should guard against the "vanity of vanities" that Ecclesiastes is pretty explicit to say will waste our lives.

So, what is the Almost Amish way? Because we're all starting at a different point, it will probably look different for each of us. For example, while speaking at a church in Texas, Matthew met a woman who admitted to spending three hours in front of the mirror each morning. Maybe it doesn't take you that long to get out the door, but we could try cutting back our grooming routine by 25 percent. And emptying a drawer or two in our vanities. (There's that word again!)

Organize your attic, garage, and basement

One of the positive benefits of moving every so often is that we don't store a mound of little-used stuff in our attic, garage, and basement. Each of the children has one "memory box." In addition, Clark has asked us to keep his college notebooks for a few years, until he is ready to part with them. Emma now has only one craft box, since she gave most of those things away to a first grade teacher the last time we moved. Matthew has his tools—just the bare bones for carpentry and household maintenance—and I have a few gardening supplies—nothing fancy, just a shovel, hoe, rake, gloves, and a couple of spades. The sports equipment fits in one plastic tub, and we have two well-used bikes. We own a few suitcases for travel, the pressure cooker and some canning equipment, and our root cellar/pantry to save trips to the store—that's pretty much it. The attic is for insulation, nothing else.

And while very occasionally I will miss something that Matthew has given away, mostly I am thankful that my husband prevents me from becoming a hoarder. "If someone else can use it now, why should we store it for someday?" is his frequent and much-appreciated refrain.

Let's Sum It Up

We might as well face it: what burdens most modern American homes is the accumulation of mass-produced junk, bought on impulse and paid for with credit, which either falls apart or no one uses. Even heirlooms can become clutter if we are not wise in our stewardship of them. Cluttered homes lead to cluttered lives, and cluttered lives can harm families.

Our homes reflect our values. They reflect who we are inside and what we hold most precious. If our houses are cluttered, our hearts are too. Possessions should work for us; we should not work for them. Too easily, our homes and the stuff that fills them can become false idols, tempting us to break the first of the Ten Commandments. The Amish offer a simpler, less cluttered, more sustainable way of life. We have much to learn from their example.

CHAPTER 2

TECHNOLOGY

Technology serves as a tool and does not rule as a master.

THERE ARE TWO KINDS OF PEOPLE in the world: those who make lists and those who don't. I do. Lists are useful not just at the grocery store: they organize my week, and they help clarify my thoughts.

Recently, I sat down and made a list of the things I love about our twenty-first-century technology:

1. I can work anytime, anywhere.
2. I can check e-mail anytime.
3. People get back to me immediately.
4. I can access entertainment anytime.
5. I can stay informed all the time.
6. I can get in touch with almost anyone, anytime.
7. I can buy almost anything, anytime.

8. I can multitask.

9. There's always something to do.

10. I never feel alone.

And then I made a list of what I *hate* about modern technology:

1. I can work anytime, anywhere.

2. I can check e-mail anytime.

3. People expect me to get back to them immediately.

4. I can access entertainment anytime.

5. I can stay informed all the time.

6. Almost anyone can get in touch with me anytime.

7. I can buy almost anything, anytime.

8. I can multitask.

9. There's always something to do.

10. I never feel alone.

While we may not all be list makers, I know I'm not the only one feeling this love-hate relationship with technology; millions of people share it. We love the convenience technology affords. We hate how technology is taking over our lives.

The Amish are different—famously so. They're well known for their rejection of technology, but the intention of those choices is less understood. In this chapter we'll take a look at the reasons the Amish might not find anything to love about my Top Ten list and what we can learn from their less-is-more approach to technology.

Limitations of Technology

When we think of the Amish, we often focus on the prohibitions: the Amish do not drive cars. They do not have electricity lines to their homes. They do not hook up to cable Internet or cable TV.

But, just as I saw with my lists of the pros and cons of technology, each of their restrictions on technology has a positive side as well. Not driving means walking more. No cable television means less time devoted to empty pursuits. In general, their limits are less about restricting privileges than fostering a calmer, more peaceful, healthier existence. Many of us plan expensive vacations to seek these very qualities and "get away from it all." For the Amish, it's a way of life.

Envision an orange triangular hazard sign on your computer monitor, with the word "CAUTION!" stamped in big letters. This is how I picture the Amish approach to technology. While not all technology is inherently bad, if left unchecked, technology can destabilize communities and amplify worldly messages. Instead of priding themselves on being "early adopters," the Amish provide a much-needed reminder to slow down and look before taking the next technological leap. Where and why do the Amish draw boundaries, and what can we learn from them?

One of the first things you notice about Amish communities is that their homes are not hooked up to power lines. This is because the Amish do not want to be dependent on networks. The specific guidelines for the use of electricity vary from community to community. Old Order Amish, for example, forbid electricity from public utility lines but allow electricity from batteries. In some settlements, batteries are used to power calculators, fans, flashlights, copy machines, and computers. In other communities, solar energy is used to charge batteries, operate electric fences, and power household appliances. Why this distinction between power lines and batteries? Because electricity from batteries is more local and controllable; moreover, its use requires the virtues of forethought and restraint, which the Amish value highly.

This reasoning makes sense to me, but perhaps most compelling is the Amish understanding that there is no free lunch. What technology offers us in terms of convenience and connectivity will always come at a cost, and the Amish carefully count that cost. One of the costs of being linked in is our privacy. Information about the movies we watch, the music we listen to, and our buying habits—even we ourselves—become products sold to advertisers.

Many of us who live far-from-Amish lives do value our privacy, and yet we may not be aware of the implications of today's dependence on connectivity. When it comes to understanding the New Big Brother, the Amish are a step ahead of us in thinking through the costs. Each time we turn on the computer, we are unwittingly granting the government, marketers, employers, and future employers access to the most intimate details of our lives. Over the last decade, a new breed of "data miners" have created a multibillion-dollar business of buying and selling information that most of us would not share with our closest friends, let alone complete strangers. What we do with technology from our homes and offices does not always give us what the law calls a "reasonable expectation of privacy." Who can read your e-mail? Track your web-surfing history? Monitor what you are watching on TV? Log who, when, and where you call? The Amish have long understood that the price of admission for connectivity is the surrender of your privacy.

But where to draw the line? To outsiders, many Amish rules surrounding technology use can seem hypocritical. Why is it okay to power equipment from a 12-volt battery but not a 110-volt current from the public utility? Isn't it splitting hairs to forbid phone lines to the home but to allow their use elsewhere? And why ban car ownership but hire non-Amish drivers to operate cars for you?

Many apparent inconsistencies in the Amish restrictions regarding technology are resolved when the motive is understood. Consider, for instance, the Amish use of diesel generators and an inverter to power small household appliances. Generators are noisy and expensive to run; they are also less convenient. This conscious decision to make power loud, costly, and inconvenient leads people to use less of it and to live more mindfully.

The particular set of decisions the Amish make can vary from community to community. But no matter how variable some community standards may be, the intent remains constant: technology should serve as a tool, not rule as a master. By establishing boundaries and living within them, the Amish are able to preserve a traditional way of life centered on God, family, and neighbors rather than be at the mercy of technology "i-gods."

How do the Amish communities determine their boundaries? By looking to Scripture for guidance. One key touchstone is Paul's advice to the Roman people, more relevant today than ever: "Don't copy the behavior and customs of this world, but let God transform you into a new person by changing the way you think. Then you will learn to know God's will for you, which is good and pleasing and perfect" (Romans 12:2).

As the pace of change increases, we, too, would be wise to make conscious choices based on eternal wisdom rather than recklessly surfing the digital wave.

Something Amiss

No one doubts the power of technology to enable us to do astounding things today; it's so easy to revel in the power that is literally at our fingertips. Yet something is wrong, terribly wrong, about our time. We feel it, like a splinter in our hearts. There's no room for margin: we Twitter while we drive, talk while we text, and surf until we fall asleep—but even while in bed, we stay plugged in, available 24/7. People tell me they could not live without their cell phones or the Internet or e-mail—and they mean it. Yet in many ways, these technologies lead us to more disconnected—rather than connected—lives.

Can we resist these trends? Are we doomed by the Fall to live broken lives—not only in the inner sanctum of our hearts, but played out on reality TV, where viewers can vote us out of Eden?

Lots of questions, few answers. But I take that as a good sign: Jesus often teaches with questions, and living in tension often means that God is at work. C. S. Lewis says that "sometimes you do have to turn the clock back if it is telling the wrong time." If we realize that we are traveling in the wrong direction, the only sensible thing to do is to admit it and retrace our steps to where we first went wrong. As Lewis puts it, "Going back can sometimes be the quickest way forward."

Opting Out: Or, Sleeping with Your Good Ear Down

One way of "going back" is cheap, simple, and readily available: opt out. We don't have to do everything that technology enables us to do—do we? At least, not all the time? The way I look at it, as ubiquitous as smartphones and social network accounts are, we still do have a choice in how we use them. Or, as I like to put it, I can sleep with my good ear down.

You know that ringing you sometimes get in your ear when you fly, and the temporary lack of hearing? Well, ten years ago, that happened to me, only it's permanent. Flying home after attending the birth of my nephew, David, I lost most of the hearing in my left ear and gained a constant high-pitched ringing called tinnitus.

Although I still can't hear much in my left ear—hearing aids won't work for me—I've learned that deafness has its advantages: not everything is worth hearing.

Over the years, I've grown judicious about asking people to repeat something. Especially at a noisy gathering, I usually can get away with smiling and nodding my head. Although on occasion I smile and nod to some pretty strange things, this can have its upside, too—people think I'm a little daffy, and low expectations are easy to exceed.

Another advantage: if my beloved starts to snore, I can sleep with my good ear down. Who'd have thunk that the ability to tune out could add to marital bliss?

Metaphorically, I've found that putting my good ear down also can add to personal bliss. The world has grown increasingly noisy since my nephew's birth. First, Internet. Next, message boards. And then the rapid-fire onslaught: chat rooms, e-mail, IM, text messaging, iTunes, Bluetooth, YouTube, Twitter—most of these did not exist a decade ago when David was born, but they now control much of our lives, and our kids' lives. I've passed children younger than David texting as soon as they step off the school bus, not even glancing up at the trees and birds and open sky as their fingers dash across the touch pad.

Is there anything wrong with offering our ears to every available technological device? How does spending more than six hours in front of a screen each day affect a child's brain development? It's a billion-person experiment, and the initial reports are not promising: physicians, psychologists, and educators are sounding alarms about potential negative outcomes of a digitally addicted generation.

But my greatest concern is not physical, emotional, or

social—it's spiritual. How can we hear the voice of God if we are multitasking nonstop? How can we see the face of God in still waters and green pastures when we are chronically refreshing the screen? The digital generation is a distracted generation.

On the other hand, what might we gain by choosing to use less technological power than we can—just as the Amish do?

More than a quarter of the world's population is hooked up to the Internet. China has the highest total number of Internet users, with the United States and Japan having the highest percentage of users (more than 75 percent). What are they all doing?

- 2.5 billion images are uploaded to Facebook each month.
- 247 billion e-mails are sent daily. About 80 percent (some websites report up to 97 percent) of these are spam.
- 20 hours of video are uploaded to YouTube every minute, which, in terms of running time, is the equivalent of Hollywood releasing 86,000 new films each week.
- More than 50 million tweets are sent every day.

Each day! Who has the time? Teens, I guess . . .

- Teens who check social networking sites more than 10 times a day: 22 percent.

- Parents who believe kids are checking that much: 4 percent.
- Teens who admit to having a profile with a false identity: 25 percent.

How do they do it all?

- About 60 percent of Americans use the Internet and TV at the same time.
- People aged 12 to 24 are accumulating up to 23 hours of activity a day, engaging in up to 5 activities simultaneously.

Now, these statistics change quickly, and inaccuracies readily propagate on the Internet. But the general message is clear: Internet usage is huge and only getting larger.

Do you find the stats disturbing? I do. They sure seem to be saying that the Internet is taking over our lives. Here's an even more disconcerting fact: according to the Bureau of Labor Statistics, the average American spends just nine minutes per day in religious and spiritual activities. This disparity between how much time we spend with technology and how much time we spend with God says much about our priorities. I think it indicates that technology is supplanting God in our hearts and affections. We are pursuing technology with an abandon and intensity that should be reserved for God alone.

Breaking the Dependency

Matthew and I have made many conscious decisions to limit the role of technology in our personal lives. No fifty-inch plasma HDTV screens, no cable networks, no video games. We don't follow friends on Facebook or Twitter, nor do we send text messages.

Our work, however, is Internet dependent. It's easy to forget that ten years ago I could not navigate the on-ramp to the information highway; today I rarely go a day without it. But when we started our nonprofit, I made a rule for myself: no e-mail on the Sabbath. The world could be coming apart, but I do not answer e-mails on Sundays. Recently, I decided to try extending that rule to all Internet usage. One way to end a dependency, of course, is to just take a regular break from it. A day a week without Internet—how easy is that?

Not very, as it turns out. Ninety percent of the time, I use the Internet for work. But much of that remaining 10 percent happens on the weekend. It's when I look for new recipes. Or check my Netflix queue. Or do geeky Christian stuff that I don't make time for during the week, such as comparing Psalm 24 in a dozen translations. Not bad things—but not necessary things. And not things centered on anyone but myself.

On one of my first Internet-less Sabbaths, Matthew and I took a long walk down to the Kentucky River. It's a steep trail, with the downhill part coming first. Eugene Peterson, best known for *The Message*, has described his Sunday walks with his wife. They don't speak for the first hour. Matthew and I did the opposite: we talked on the way down, knowing that we'd have no breath to spare for words on the uphill return.

As we started the descent, I asked Matthew for his thoughts on Internet dependency. Matthew knelt beside a tree stump to retie his shoelace. "Well, you know how I feel about time spent on the Internet. It's kind of like incandescent lightbulbs: 10 percent useful, 90 percent wasted energy."

"Exactly! Lots of excess heat, but not much useful light."

I offered Matthew my hand as he stood up. He kept holding it as we continued down the path to the river: "Here's the question I ask myself: *When Jesus returns, do I want him to find me asleep—wasting hours on YouTube or playing Spider Solitaire?* No. I'd rather have him find me sharing a meal. Listening to a friend. Planting a tree."

I squeezed his hand, then let go. "Ditto." Am I lucky to be married to this guy, or what?

After skipping some stones on the river—Matthew scored nine skips to my three—we headed back up, this time on a trail that demands walking single file. Matthew took the lead, I followed. Even if the trail were wider, it would be difficult to speak—the trail is that steep.

So, instead, I reflected on our conversation. I prayed that I would not be like an inefficient lightbulb, wasting 90 percent of my life on e-mail and Internet—or any other interesting but largely empty pursuit. I prayed that God would help me be a light on the hill and that I wouldn't hide that light under a basket out of habit or laziness or fear.

I prayed that I would learn to keep my mouth shut and listen—to God, to my husband, to friends and family. For the moment, I simply listened to the squirrels scampering along the branch highway above our heads, the woodpecker searching for insects in a dead tree, and the snapping of twigs as we walked out of the dense woods and into the late afternoon sunshine.

After we got home from the walk, I intentionally spent an hour in silence. Not reading. Not listening to music. Not on the computer. Simply shifting from a human *doing* to a human *being*.

The Almost Amish Way: Embrace Technology with Caution

Of course, fasting from the Internet—or from anything else that we find has distracted us or captured too much of our attention—is based on the biblical principle to keep the focus on God. I like to think of temporary fasts as a try-before-you-buy way to approximate the Amish experience—tasting the benefits of that lifestyle without adopting it wholesale. Here are some other practical tips for making conscious choices about technology:

"Turn off your cell phones, please . . ."

We all know how distracting it is to hear a cell phone go off in a formal meeting, whether at work or church or anywhere else. But what about in more-casual gatherings? We have an acquaintance who is truly wonderful, save one thing: he is addicted to his cell phone. This man is a devoted husband and father; he is great about initiating friendly gatherings and is fully committed to the ministry he leads. However, every time we are with him, his phone buzzes almost constantly. We are not the only ones to notice this almost Pavlovian response to the cell phone. His wife and friends tease him about it, but the humor is tinged with frustration.

Unfortunately, this friend's cell phone tether is not an anomaly. I remember going out to dinner with some young music-industry leaders. Every few minutes, one of them wandered off, cell phone in hand, to answer a call or return a text or check an incoming e-mail. The conversation was disjointed, and the meal we shared was anything but relaxing.

If you cannot go cold turkey, start by setting healthy boundaries. The Amish often joke that visiting is their "national pastime." What a lovely concept, and a living statement on the priority they place on presence. Because children do not lead the family, adults can actually sit, uninterrupted, and talk. The phone does not buzz, the computer does not beep, and the carpool horn does not bellow. By drawing boundaries, the Amish have access to something technology can only loosely mimic: real-time-and-space connection.

What are some first steps in that direction? Well, if the dentist's office can request that we turn off cell phones, so can you. Make mealtime a phone-free time. Tell teens to turn off the cell phones after 8:00 p.m., or whatever time you decide is reasonable, and be sure that it happens. Think long and hard before giving your youngster or tween a cell phone at all; generations upon generations have gotten along just fine without them, and we may later learn that they contribute to health issues in developing bodies. But make sure you remove the plank from your own eye first. Children learn more from what we do than what we say. Only when our own vision is clear can we help others remove the specks from their eyes.

To go a little further, you might try putting a few limits on your usage, in order to reduce temptation to always be available to everyone you know and maybe even some people you don't know. For example, I have a cell phone, but I keep the list of contacts to about a dozen names—only family and a couple of close friends have my number. I don't even know how to send a text message. And thus far, I have also resisted being "upgraded" to a smartphone: being hooked to the Internet anywhere, anytime is just too seductive for me, and an ounce of prevention is worth many gigabytes of cure. "Lead us not into temptation, but deliver us from evil: For thine is the kingdom, and the power, and the glory" (Matthew 6:13, KJV). Amen!

Don't get me wrong: cell phones are not intrinsically evil, any more than an old-fashioned land line is intrinsically evil. Being available to answer the phone at all times, however, can make you its slave, and that can interfere with real-time-and-space relationships with God, family, and friends.

Limit (or eliminate) TV

Even before the American Academy of Pediatrics came out with their recommendation of no TV before age two (and extremely limited before age five), my husband made it clear that our preschoolers should not watch TV. We owned only one television, which we kept behind a cabinet door in the family room. The family room was connected in an L-shape to the kitchen, so no one could watch TV without everyone knowing.

To further limit TV use, we prerecorded shows—and then we chose when the children would watch them. I don't think it's terrible for school-aged kids to watch a thirty-minute program every so often—especially during the bewitching hour when Mom is preparing dinner. However, let's call a spade a spade. I was using the TV as an electronic babysitter. If I had been a better disciplinarian, or a little less tired, I would have encouraged them to do something more creative with their time. Turning on the tube to keep the peace was a cop-out.

Our family has been without TV for more than a decade. I believe that this is one of the best gifts we have given to ourselves and to our kids. Matthew and I enjoy watching movies now, but we are selective. Not having cable television removes the temptation to channel surf. When we watch a film or documentary, it is a conscious choice—something we do together or with the kids and their friends.

Again, TV is not inherently bad, but if it is interfering in your relationships with God, family, and friends, then you need to hit the pause button. These days, such restrictions should include computers and phones as well—anything that can provide on-demand, solitary entertainment. Establish clear boundaries for children. Keep TVs out of the bedrooms, where you cannot monitor what and how much they are watching. And set a good example yourself. Falling asleep with the twenty-four-hour news show on or snoring through a football game wastes energy and dampens the love life. If these restrictions seem harsh, consider their upsides: calmer homes, healthier kids, and more meaningful couple time. That's the goal—isn't it worth it?

Cut back on computer games

I have played a computer game only once, for less than two minutes. The game was Tetris, and I probably scored lower than any neophyte in gaming history. I stunk. But sour grapes is not why I quit. I just did not see the point: I'd rather answer a client satisfaction survey on our homeowner's insurance policy. In my analog brain, the allure of computer games just does not compute.

I am, once again, in the minority. Nearly 70 percent of US households include gamers. Forty percent of these are women. Among families in which one or more parents play computer games, 93 percent of their children do too.

Can video games fuel health problems? Yes, according to a recent report in the medical journal *Pediatrics*. The study tracked two thousand elementary- and middle-school-aged children for two years. The conclusion: the greater the frequency of gaming, the greater the possibility of reduced social skills, poor school performance, and depression. When their gaming addiction was stopped, the depression, anxiety, and social phobias got better.

And what about physical health? A recent study conducted by the World Health Organization cites video games as a major contributor to childhood obesity. Forty-two million children under the age of five are now overweight or obese; these children are more likely to remain obese into adulthood and to develop diabetes and cardiovascular diseases at a younger age. The report cites "sedentary lifestyle," including computer games and television, as a key factor. Only 25 percent of boys and 15 percent of girls in the thirty-four countries surveyed are getting enough exercise. Even here in the United States, our youth are not as fit as we might think. Despite many opportunities to participate in organized sports, a recent survey found only 15 percent of American high school students meet the Centers for Disease Control and Prevention's recommendations for aerobic activity.

After one of our workshops on simplicity and creation care, a young mother approached me. Her second grader's birthday was coming up, and he had asked for the latest and greatest computer game. The mom thought her son already spent way too much time on the computer, but she felt torn. "All his friends are playing it. I don't want him to feel ostracized."

My response: don't buy it. Don't buy into the necessity of

fitting in. Don't buy into the social pressure. No eight-year-old is (or should be) able to walk to the store by himself and plunk down a hundred bucks for a video game. Parents do have a say. In the long run, as with so many other parental decisions, thoughtfully answering "no" can be the most loving gift we can offer. We can give our children a chance to drink deeply of life instead of always settling for shallow pleasures.

How to begin? First and foremost, set an example. Keep games out of the home. If and when they are used, limit them to thirty minutes or less per day. Avoid them completely on the Sabbath. And carefully monitor their content—even if you don't believe in a connection between virtual violence and the real thing, blowing up people for entertainment is the inverse of the "pure, and lovely, and admirable" that the apostle Paul said we should seek. Instead, substitute activities that are "excellent and worthy of praise," such as spending time outdoors enjoying God's creation. (See Philippians 4:8 for more entertainment guidelines.)

Except for a few games that came preloaded on our computer, Matthew and I have never purchased a video game or game console. The same goes for our children. What did they do instead of playing video games or watching TV? On rainy days they used wooden block sets to build cathedrals with working catapults and trapdoors; created obstacle courses out of dominoes lined up end to end; wrote books and illustrated them; developed scripts, made costumes, and put on plays. On sunny days, they climbed trees, built forts, traipsed along creek beds, explored salt marshes, gathered sea glass, and dug for buried treasure. In below-freezing temperatures, we had to call them in from building snow tunnels with the neighborhood kids. They often got so busy playing outdoors they would forget to come home to eat. And books—well, let's just say that Beth, the children's librarian, was one of our dearest friends. She enthusiastically recommended old classics and saved new books just for my children, always willing to discuss in great detail their evolving literary tastes. "I'm bored" was never a complaint as long as there were good books to read, a sketch pad and drawing pencil, or a tree to climb. It *is* possible to raise kids in twenty-first-century America without Xbox, PlayStation, or Wii. We *can* live in the world without conforming to its ways—and enjoy ourselves in the process.

Reduce incoming e-mail

Winston Churchill is a family hero of ours. At the dinner table, Clark does a pretty good imitation of the great orator. One of my favorite Churchill quotations is, "I am all for your using machines, but do not let them use you."

If there is one area where I am at the mercy of machines, it is e-mail. Because I rarely use the phone and do not text message, nearly all my work communications are done via e-mail. My justification: e-mail keeps my life quieter. Without it, our phone would be ringing constantly. But too much of even a good thing can be bad.

A couple of years ago, I accidentally discovered that I had 7,856 e-mails in my in-box. When I confessed my e-mail problem to a friend, she said it was the most over-filled mail-box she had ever heard of. "I know a couple of people who have a thousand or even two thousand e-mails, but this is crazy. Your in-box is officially out of control."

I have since changed over to an e-mail system with better search capabilities. But I have also taken some defensive actions. First, I unsubscribed from every group list that I can live without—which is almost all of them. This took some time and continues to require ongoing vigilance, but the pay-off is huge—it has reduced my incoming e-mail by nearly half.

Second, I stopped opening anything that even vaguely resembles spam or junk mail. If I don't open paper-based junk mail, why should I open virtual junk mail? Opening junk mail is a distraction and a waste of time.

Deleting e-mails is among my top five, least-favorite duties—I'd far rather clean toilets. But someone has got to take out the trash and dump the compost, even in cyberspace.

Approach social media with caution

Everywhere I travel, I hear people tout the merits of social media. And, as with other applications of technology, some of this praise is deserved. Social media provide a way to con-nect, to create community, to share information, and to pro-mote good causes. But if there is one area of technology that gives me the heebie-jeebies, it is social media. Why? Because the price we pay is privacy.

Every time we log on, Father Internet is collecting

information about how many avocados we purchase, what library books we check out, which Netflix videos we rate at five stars, how long we linger on a web page, and where we spend, invest, and give away our money. The most disconcerting part, though, is that no one forces us to participate. Voluntarily, we are giving away our privacy. I've heard people argue that if you have nothing to hide, what's the big deal?

My concern is not whether people have anything to hide— Jesus will shine a light on everything in the end—it's about humility, modesty, and discretion. By now we have all heard a story like that of the middle-school girl who receives a bare-chested text photo from a guy she likes, responds with a nude of herself . . . and finds it sent to hundreds of other "friends" on Facebook in no time. Rumors fly, school authorities are noti-fied, the shocked parents are called in, the girl is alienated and transfers schools. Although she deeply regrets her impulsive (and foolish) action, the label follows her and she is scarred.

Severe cases, such as the gay boy who is outed on Facebook and ends up committing suicide, make the headlines. But many adults, like the middle-school girl's parents, are clueless about what is happening in their own homes and neighbor-hoods. Other adults are participating themselves. As recent technology-assisted sex scandals among politicians attest, wealth, social status, or education level does not protect us from the dark side of ourselves in any situation, whether online or off.

Of course, incidents of rude, crude, tactless, impulsive, reckless, and thoughtless behavior are everywhere; social media simply have the capacity to spread these actions further and faster. As I mentioned earlier in this chapter, the Amish were wary of networks long before the cyber variety came to be, but their caution makes a lot of sense in light of the social ills allowed to metastasize via social networks. For instance, the Amish are very intentional about visiting neighbors and developing strong community ties. Such face-to-face relationships can be weakened by hyperconnectivity in the virtual world. Social media quickly become unsocial means of communication when all your friends live within horse and buggy distance.

Another hazard of social media is TMI: teens and adults alike are being crushed by Too Much Information. We share too much. We receive too much. Then we expect some digital trash compactor to squash it all into a neat little cyber package and make it go away.

Amish culture is the inverse of TMI. For the most part, the Amish are a people of few words. They hold their tongues in obedience to God's Word. Allowing biblical wisdom to give us pause when we engage in social media is one way to start becoming Almost Amish.

- Proverbs 18:2—"Fools have no interest in understanding; they only want to air their own opinions." (Blog posts, comments on blogs?)
- Proverbs 18:21—"The tongue can bring death or life; those who love to talk will reap the consequences." (Regrettable tweets?)

- Proverbs 25:23—"As surely as a north wind brings rain, so a gossiping tongue causes anger!" (Celebrity worship, scandal mongers?)
- Proverbs 13:3—"Those who control their tongue will have a long life; opening your mouth can ruin everything." (Political brouhaha?)
- Proverbs 15:4—"Gentle words are a tree of life; a deceitful tongue crushes the spirit." (Middle-school Facebook?)

The intent behind such admonitions, not only in Proverbs but throughout the Bible, is consistent: loose lips sink ships. Or, as a wise Amish proverb puts it, "Blessed are those who have nothing to say and cannot be persuaded to say it."

Let's Sum It Up

When asked who they think is the greatest living writer today, both my son and husband answered the same: Mark Helprin, master of many genres (if you have not read his *Swan Lake* trilogy, you should, even without a child to sit on your lap). Among many other things, Helprin has written a manifesto titled *Digital Barbarism*, in which he warns against worshiping at millions of man-made altars. We allow even "the tiniest of these, that fit in our ears or that we can barely operate with our thumbs," to exercise control over us. "Who is servant, and who is master?" he asks.

It's a timely question with eternal implications. In Helprin's view, there is hope that we can control the role of technology in our lives through an act of will—"the will to do without, the will to have less, the refusal to model human nature after the mechanical."

This "will" implies conscious choice. When we face the fact that technology is neither fully good nor fully bad, but a tool to be used at our disposal, it becomes easier to see that we can exercise choice over how we use it. Temptation comes in many disguises. We love the allure of convenience; we hate the tyranny of a digital dependency. But as with any other good, a sober-minded faith seeks to use technology in an appropriate way; we should not become either a slave or a glutton on account of it. The Amish show us how restrained use of technology can allow more time for others and result in healthier, richer lives. As we use the paradoxical teachings of Christ as our model, setting boundaries with technology can be one of the most liberating things we can do.

CHAPTER 3

FINANCES

Saving more and spending less bring financial peace.

OUR ANNIVERSARY and my birthday are just five days apart. While gifts have never been my primary "love language," since we downsized I've made an even greater effort to resist the temptation to reclutter. In our town house, there's simply not a lot of room for extra anything. One result is that I rarely ask for presents, but this year was special—our thirtieth anniversary. We had just moved downtown and I wanted bike baskets to help tote the groceries, so I asked Matthew to equip my bike, which was nearly two decades old and had never had a tune-up, for urban commuting.

Matthew walked my bike over to the local shop and ordered the works—high-tech commuter bags, a water bottle holder, the kickstand that I had never gotten around to putting on—price was no object. When it was ready, he asked me to come take a look, excited to show me all the new features. Then he encouraged me to take it for a spin to make sure everything worked okay.

After Matthew adjusted my helmet (once an ER doc, always an ER doc), I rode the five blocks to Emma's apartment. The bike practically drove itself—the gears switching more smoothly than they had in years, the brakes gliding me to a gentle stop minus the usual blue-jay screech. I parked the bike next to Emma's door and ran upstairs. We chatted for a few minutes. When I came back down, the space where I had left the bike was empty. My newly restored bicycle was gone—vamoosed—stolen on its maiden voyage.

After my initial disbelief—it's hard to take in that the gift you were given just a few minutes ago is now gone—and, yes, some decidedly *not* turning-the-other-cheek-type thoughts, I said a quick prayer for the person who stole the bike, hoping it was someone who needed it more than I did. Apparently the thief already had a helmet: mine was left resting on the top of Emma's recycling bin.

When I called the police, they asked if the bike shop had recorded the bike's serial number. Matthew handed me the receipt, to see if it had the serial number on it, and so I learned that—in his enthusiasm to please me with a special gift—he had spent more on the tune-up and accessories than I had originally paid for the bicycle.

I learned several lessons that day:

1. Saying a quick "hi" to your daughter—or anyone you love—often takes longer than expected.
2. If you never did like the bright purple color of your bike, add some fancy baskets and water bottles, and the problem will disappear.
3. God won't strike you down for wishing a severe outbreak of acne on someone who does you wrong.
4. After venting vindictive thoughts, it feels good to pray.
5. Everything belongs to God.
6. Nothing of any real value can be taken away.
7. It really is the thought behind the gift that counts.
8. The best things in life are free (and most clichés are true).
9. You can purchase a replacement bike on craigslist with all the fancy bells and whistles for less than you would spend on accessories alone at a bike shop—in a color that is decidedly not purple.
10. Life works best with God behind the wheel, even (especially!) when it doesn't seem that way at the time.

In the end, I felt sorrier for Matthew than for myself. He had been so keyed up about the gift, and then thirty minutes later it was gone.

While having the bike stolen certainly was not Matthew's intention, it was actually the best birthday present that he could have given me: a yearly reminder that real security comes from God alone.

Money Matters: How "Amish" Are You?

Although Matthew and I have been simplifying our lives for some time now, we still have much to learn from Amish principles of financial simplicity. If you're looking to make changes, it's important to know where you're starting from. Before we discuss how the Amish handle money matters, answer (honestly!) the following questions:

Stuff

Do you wish your home were less cluttered?

Do you have too many clothes in your closet?

Do you have recreational or sports equipment sitting in your basement or garage that is rarely used?

Do you own more high-tech gadgets than you need?

Are you renting a storage unit?

Debt and spending

If you use credit cards, have you ever paid less than the full balance?

Have you ever bought something on credit that will be worth less in a year?

Do you give away at least 10 percent of your earnings?

Are you depending exclusively on Social Security to provide for your old age?

Spending

> Does anyone in your household shop recreationally—
> for example, go to the mall with no specific purchase
> in mind?
> Do you ever buy gifts out of guilt or obligation?
> Do you make major purchases without waiting a month
> to determine if you really need them?
> Do you ever feel that you spent more than you should
> at Christmas?
> Have you ever hidden a purchase from your spouse or
> bought something to get back at him or her?

If you answered "yes" to more than a few of these questions, you are not alone; so does our nation as a whole. It's no secret that we are struggling under a weighty debt burden in our country, but are we as individuals doing any better? We all have much to learn from our Amish friends—so let's take a look at how they view finances.

Survival of the Thriftiest

During the recent economic downturn, a number of newspapers and magazines ran stories on how the Amish have not only survived, but thrived. At first I thought the Amish might have been helped by an unfair tax advantage, but it turns out that they are responsible for income, property, and sales taxes, just like the rest of us. The only exception is Social Security: they are exempted from paying in because they don't accept government aid for their elderly. Why, then, is the five-year success rate of Amish businesses more than 90 percent, almost double the national average? The answer is simple: frugality. Amish monetary policy—little things matter; buy what you need, not what you want; waste not, want not—can make the difference between success or failure, especially in difficult economic times.

Thrift, delayed gratification, self-control, and sharing are the hallmarks of Amish finances. But what's interesting to me is that these principles are based on a worldview of abundance rather than scarcity. When a couple gets married, friends come over to help paint the house. If someone loses a job, neighbors share produce from their gardens. When a family faces unexpected medical bills, the community takes up a special collection.

What I find most beguiling about Amish finances is the underlying principle of humility. They do not buy things to impress or to draw attention to themselves or to win love. They understand that every single thing on earth is a gift from God, meant to be shared with others. And they act from the certainty that the most important things in life cannot be found at "the mall that has it all."

Back to Basics

How did the Amish get so smart about money? They learned from the bestselling financial self-help book of all time, the Bible. God has given us more than eight hundred Scriptures on money and its proper role in our lives. Below are a few of the principles that guide Amish finances.

- Work hard. "Lazy people want much but get little, but those who work hard will prosper." (Proverbs 13:4)
- Give God your firstfruits. "Honor the LORD with your wealth and with the best part of everything you produce." (Proverbs 3:9)
- Spend wisely. "The wise have wealth and luxury, but fools spend whatever they get." (Proverbs 21:20)
- Be honest in all dealings. "The LORD detests the use of dishonest scales, but he delights in accurate weights." (Proverbs 11:1)
- Guard against greed. "[Jesus] said, 'Beware! Guard against every kind of greed. Life is not measured by how much you own.'" (Luke 12:15)
- Be prudent. "Don't begin until you count the cost. For who would begin construction of a building without first calculating the cost to see if there is enough money to finish it?" (Luke 14:28)
- Don't become a slave to debt. "Just as the rich rule the poor, so the borrower is servant to the lender." (Proverbs 22:7)
- Save for the lean times. "Have them gather all the food produced in the good years that are just ahead and bring it to Pharaoh's storehouses. Store it away, and guard it so there will be food in the cities. That

way there will be enough to eat when the seven years of famine come." (Genesis 41:35-36)
- Provide for your family, young and old. "Those who won't care for their relatives, especially those in their own household, have denied the true faith. Such people are worse than unbelievers." (1 Timothy 5:8)
- Give generously. "God loves a person who gives cheerfully." (2 Corinthians 9:7)

Note the similarities of these biblical principles with the wisdom found in the Amish proverbs listed below. You may be familiar with some already.

- We live simply so others may simply live.
- Use it up, wear it out, make do, or do without.
- Take all you want, eat all you take.
- He who has no money is poor; he who has nothing but money is even poorer.
- There are no degrees of honesty.
- A man is rich in proportion to the things he can afford to leave alone.
- If you are true to your faith, there are things you give up for your faith.
- Opportunity may knock once, but temptation bangs at your door forever.
- Generosity leaves a much better taste than stinginess.
- Before we can pray "Thy Kingdom come," we must first pray "My Kingdom go."

NANCY SLEETH

The Reverend Martin Luther King takes this last Amish proverb even one step further. King considered money an equal opportunity taskmaster: it can enslave the oppressor as much as the oppressed. In a prescient sermon, "The False God of Money," King warns us about making money the center of our lives. One of King's fears was that people had become more concerned with "making a living than making a life." With e-mail, text messaging, and cell phone tethers still the stuff of science fiction, MLK's 1953 message reads like a fax to the future.

Tim Keller of Redeemer Church in Manhattan draws a similar conclusion in his book *Counterfeit Gods*: An idol is "anything more important to you than God, anything that absorbs your heart and imagination more than God, anything you seek to give you what only God can give." Our finances can be just such an idol. The human heart takes good things— like a successful career, money in the bank, and the objects we purchase—and turns them into "ultimate things."

The Amish are cautious about making money an ultimate thing. We, too, should be wary of any false idols that dominate our thoughts, minds, and actions.

Money Worship

The Bible is full of characters led astray by worship of the Almighty Dollar: among others, King Belshazzar at the feast, the money changers on Solomon's Porch, and Ananias and his wife—who hid money from the apostles—come to mind.

The ultimate example of a money worshiper, however, has got to be Judas Iscariot. Why? Because he was intimate with the living, breathing Jesus. He watched him feed crowds of thousands. He saw Jesus walk on water and calm the storm. Even with his best buddy restoring sight to the blind and bringing people back from the dead, Judas succumbed to greed.

John describes the scene as follows:

> Six days before the Passover celebration began, Jesus arrived in Bethany, the home of Lazarus—the man he had raised from the dead. A dinner was prepared in Jesus' honor. Martha served, and Lazarus was among those who ate with him. Then Mary took a twelve-ounce jar of expensive perfume made from essence of nard, and she anointed Jesus' feet with it, wiping his feet with her hair. The house was filled with the fragrance.
>
> But Judas Iscariot, the disciple who would soon betray him, said, "That perfume was worth a year's wages. It should have been sold and the money given to the poor." Not that he cared for the poor—he was a thief, and since he was in charge of the disciples' money, he often stole some for himself.
> (JOHN 12:1-6)

John is clear: Judas does not sell out Jesus on impulse. His betrayal is not an aberration of character. Rather, Judas has been dipping into the till for quite some time. He is the bookkeeper, cooking the books for his own benefit. The objection he raises to the anointing is a red herring, a distraction: he's looking for an excuse to start a fight. Judas wants to find fault with his boss to justify his own greed.

To our modern ears, it sounds like Judas got in over his head and is running scared. He knows the impending IRS audit will bring his crimes to light, and he wants to get rid of the examiner before the examiner exposes him. Accepting thirty pieces of silver for the life of the only sinless man cannot make sense until we understand this as the final, desperate act of a habitual money worshiper.

The Almost Amish Way: Save More, Spend Less

Some people are naturally less materialistic than others, while some of us really have to work at it. My son and daughter-in-law, for example, don't have to fight the desire to want things—they simply don't have that desire. But most of us could use a little help with the battle. Wherever you're starting from, keep in mind that total money makeovers don't happen overnight. First the heart changes, then the actions follow. The key is to take that first step. Below are some Almost Amish tips to help you get started.

Don't buy things you don't need

The Amish are frugal. They save at a higher rate than the rest of society and don't get over their heads in debt. One of the main reasons is that they do not buy things they don't need.

Many family homes, and family relationships, are being buried in stuff. Our closets overflow, our attics bulge, and our basements runneth over—so we rent storage units to shelter things we never use. We own five extension cords but can't locate any of them when we need one—so we head to the hardware store and purchase another.

You probably have encountered couples who compete in spending wars: if the husband purchases golf clubs, the wife retaliates by buying $300 shoes. If little Sally gets an extravagant dollhouse that she uses twice before growing bored, then Johnny deserves a new computer game. It's a nonstop battle in which everyone ends up the loser.

Whatever the reason, careless spending adds up. On average, Americans consume twice as much as we did fifty years ago. (We also see more advertisements in one year than the average person fifty years ago saw in a lifetime—do you think there is any connection between commercials and consumption?) But according to many accounts, including Annie Leonard's *The Story of Stuff*, our national happiness peaked sometime in the 1950s. We own more, but we enjoy it less.

Without intending to, we often pass along this discontent to our children. Consider, for example, chores and allowances. The Amish expect their children to contribute to the family, so they do not pay their children for chores or give them allowances. When Clark and Emma were growing up, Matthew and I adopted a similar approach. We did not pay our kids for weeding the garden or chopping kindling, nor did we give them a weekly allowance. Between birthdays, holidays, and summer jobs, they had access to money and practiced managing it. By God's grace, neither wanted much, and we never had to deal with temper tantrums at the toy store. They knew better than to even ask: if the item was trendy, poorly manufactured, or did not add beauty to our life, the answer was consistently "no." Our approach was not the norm in our neighborhood, but it seems to have paid off. As young adults, both of our children are very responsible with money. They spend little and live lightly.

We have friends with young children who have a birthday tradition that I admire—an excellent on-ramp for parents who want to tone down the feelings of entitlement so many of our children seem to have. As birthdays approach, they ask their children to select three charities for relatives to give to in lieu of presents. They focus on needs that are local and tangible—neighborhood kids who get blisters because their sneakers don't fit or children who get in trouble because they cannot afford collared shirts in the prescribed school colors. The result is children who learn to give as well as get.

I have another friend who was struggling with Christmas overload. She is a stay-at-home mom and her husband is an educator, so their budget is limited. But even if they had unlimited finances, they don't want to fill their home with plastic-fantastic toys that get broken or forgotten a month later. So the family adopted a three-present rule: one for fun, one for learning, and one to bring them closer to God. Getting the extended family to understand their less-is-more approach to Christmas has not been a smooth process, but each year it gets easier. In the long run, we would be doing our kids (and grandkids) a favor if we made celebrations less about toys and more about traditions.

Here's some get-rich-slow advice: if you are just starting out, stay off the possession treadmill. Don't be like the old lady who swallowed the fly—working more hours to pay for bigger houses with more closets and larger basements—and then renting a storage unit to hide the overflow. One day God will shine a spotlight on all of it, including the dresser in the attic you are saving for "someday" instead of allowing a needier family to be using it now.

If you already own too much stuff, start by cleaning out just one closet each weekend. If sorting through the whole basement or garage is too overwhelming, focus on a single area—tools this week, sentimental stuff next week, toys the following week, and so on. Once you clean out, follow this simple rule—give away one item for every nonperishable item you bring in. If you get really ambitious, give away two!

Stay out of debt

All this stuff costs—a lot. We are a nation of spenders, addicted to debt. Some 40 percent of American families spend more than they earn each year. About 60 percent of active credit card accounts are not paid off monthly. Among those who carry a balance, the average credit card debt is nearly $16,000 per household. The average interest rate on credit cards is currently 18.9 percent. And 25 percent of families have no reserves—no retirement account, no bank savings. When the unexpected happens—such as illness or a medical emergency—there is no cushion, and declaring bankruptcy is the result.

Medical expenses are astronomical, but it's not just patients who are affected. According to the Association of American Medical Colleges, the average medical school student graduates with more than $155,000 in student loans—and that figure keeps rising. Even back when Matthew was in medical school, we knew classmates who were more than $300,000 in debt.

Matthew had one colleague who cared deeply about his patients but had no money sense. He made a lot of money, but spent even more. Because doctors "give up" about a decade of their lives in medical school and residency, often working eighty hours per week, they seek rewards later in life through expensive vacations and fancy toys. Between student loans and out-of-control spending habits, our doctor friend fell so deeply into debt that he had to sell his house and file for bankruptcy.

Matthew and I came to marriage from very different backgrounds, but one area we never argue about is debt: we both have zero tolerance. When Matthew graduated from medical school, we immediately began paying off his relatively modest student loans. While our friends went on vacations, we used his meager residency salary to pay down his debt. By the end of his first year of practice, the student loans were completely paid off.

A year later, we took out a mortgage to build our home.

With Matthew's prodding, we chose a fifteen-year mortgage over the usual thirty years—and then made extra payments so we could pay it off early. While we were grateful for God's provision of an income that allowed us to do this—for some, extra payments are simply not an option—we could have chosen to do other things with that money. Instead, we chose to make paying off this debt a priority, clearing the entire balance in less than four years. We have always saved to pay for cars in cash, and though we do have credit cards, we always pay off the monthly balance in full—using them as a convenient tool rather than a source of loans.

Matthew and I have had some rich years, but we've shared plenty of rice-and-beans years too. No matter the size of the checking balance, the Almost Amish approach is to never pay less than the full balance on credit cards. Once you owe credit card debt, it snowballs quickly.

If you do incur debt, the important thing is to dedicate yourself to paying it off quickly, whatever your approach may be. For example, to reverse the credit card debt cycle, some financial gurus urge first paying off the card with the smallest balance, then working your way up. Others urge you to start with the credit card that charges the highest interest. The former method gives a quick psychological boost; the latter makes more mathematical sense. Which method is best? It depends on your personality and the specifics of your obligations. Any system will work if you free up every possible dollar toward paying down debt and if all members of the family doggedly stick with the plan.

Save (a lot) more

As we get out of debt, we also need to start saving—a lot more than we are now. People in China, for instance, save over 20 percent of their income. According to the OECD (Organisation for Economic Co-operation and Development), Germany, France, and Spain all save around 15 percent. The savings rate in the United States is currently less than 4 percent—better than in 2005, when our savings rate dipped below zero (spending more than we were making), but still not nearly enough to provide for education, medical expenses, and retirement.

What about the Amish? While specific information is difficult to come by, one clue is the health of banks that do business with the Amish. According to a story that ran on National Public Radio after the 2008 financial meltdown, local banks that serve the Amish fared better than most. For example, at HomeTowne Heritage Bank in Lancaster County, Pennsylvania, the vast majority of customers are Amish—which is to say that they are savers, not spenders. They avoid expensive meals out and high-tech entertainment centers, steer clear of automobiles and gas-guzzling farm equipment, and are generally known for a frugal and simple approach to life. About the only time the Amish use credit is when they buy a farm. When many banks were imploding in 2008, HomeTowne bank had its best year yet.

One reason for the success of the Amish: they do business the old-fashioned way. Because they don't drive cars or bank online, the loan officers come to them. They have worked with the same families for decades. They know the farmers behind the farms. They know their character. For the Amish, missing a payment would bring shame not only on themselves but on the extended family and the community as a whole.

It's interesting to note that subprime loans, which led to so much trouble in the general market, are virtually nonexistent among the Amish. The local bank makes the loans and services them for the duration. Even if banks that deal with the Amish had wanted to, they could not have "bundled" their mortgages and resold them in the secondary money market. In order for a mortgage to be securitized, a home has to have electricity and be covered by traditional insurance. Because the Amish live literally off the grid and do not purchase homeowner's insurance, their loans could not be sold. The primary insurance among the Amish: a commitment to help one another.

Give generously

When Matthew and I first married, he was just starting college and my job paid $15,000 per year. Even in those frugal times, we followed a general rule of thirds: spend a third, save a third, and give a third to Uncle Sam, friends in need, or charity.

Thirty years later, we still generally adhere to our "rule of thirds." Because we are in a higher tax bracket, Uncle Sam takes a bigger bite out of our giving portion, so each January, I figure out how much Matthew and I expect to earn in the coming year and I deposit a lump sum of money in a separate giving account. For us, it works best to make the full deposit in the beginning of the year, but I know others who set aside their giving-account money monthly or quarterly. While a far cry from the "sell everything and give it to the poor" advice that Jesus offers to the rich young man, setting aside the money up front has made our giving more joyful.

Each of us has things that come easily to us on our faith journey. Forgiveness, for example, comes easily for me, but generosity is harder. The dark side of frugality, of course, is stinginess—an area where I seek God's help. It seems natural to Matthew to give the shirt off his back. I have seen him do it, literally.

Matthew loves to write checks from the giving account, but he does not stop there. If something is not bolted down in our house, he considers it fair game. Books, stereos, clothes, furniture, food—I never know what will be here today and given away tomorrow. Throughout the week, I see him reaching into his pocket and handing whatever cash he has to whomever. While I have to admit that his generosity can be disconcerting at times, I have grown not only to tolerate it but to encourage it. My husband is the most generous person I know, and even after three decades of marriage, I have much to learn from his example.

I know a young woman who recently completed a doctoral degree in philanthropic studies. She bought the textbooks and went to classes and everything! The best book on the subject, however, is more than two millennia old. Scripture is replete with guidance on giving. Here's the SparkNotes version: God owns everything. We are his appointed managers. Because God is so generous in sharing everything he owns with us, we should share with others, especially those in need.

Jesus talks a lot about money, and he gives many specific principles to follow. His overarching intent is clear: going to church, attending Bible study, and doing our quiet times are all for naught if we do not care for the widows and orphans among us. When Jesus rebukes the Pharisees, he is reminding us, *today*, that our praise songs mean nothing if we fail to care for the poor. As the apostle James says, faith without works is dead. Generous acts flow from a grateful heart.

Although the Bible includes scores of passages about money, I find the most compelling reminders in the parable of the ten lepers. The story begins with Jesus heading toward Jerusalem. A group of lepers call out, "Jesus, Master, have mercy on us!"

> [Jesus] looked at them and said, "Go show yourselves to the priests." And as they went, they were cleansed of their leprosy.
>
> One of them, when he saw that he was healed, came back to Jesus, shouting, "Praise God!" He fell to the ground at Jesus' feet, thanking him for what he had done. This man was a Samaritan.

Jesus asked, "Didn't I heal ten men? Where are
the other nine? Has no one returned to give glory
to God except this foreigner?" And Jesus said to the
man, "Stand up and go. Your faith has healed you."
LUKE 17:14-19

Clearly, all ten of these social outcasts have faith. All ten shout, "Hey, Doc!" All ten believe that Jesus, the Great Physician, can help them. And all ten follow the doctor's orders, trusting that his prescription will work.

How, then, is the Samaritan's faith different? What sets the Samaritan apart is his acknowledgment that everything good comes from God. Faith, in the case of the foreigner, flows from gratitude. The Samaritan has been restored from the inside out. In the process of healing his skin, Jesus has also healed his heart.

What does this parable have to do with giving? Generosity, like gratitude, heals from the inside out. It begins with an acknowledgment that all good comes from God. Every cent we have, everything we own, belongs to the Lord. It is a privilege to serve as his appointed agents. Our job is to look for giving opportunities. When such occasions come our way, we get back far more than we give.

The Amish understand this attitude of giving out of gratitude. In times of scarcity or misfortune, everyone pitches in. Those with more take care of those with less. The community becomes the face of God's grace.

Make investments that reflect your values

So far we have covered spending, saving, and giving, but what about investing? Are there biblically based Amish principles for investing money?

Most of us are familiar with the parable of the three servants (Matthew 25:14-30), in which the servant who buries his money is rebuked, but the one who invests it wisely in the Kingdom is rewarded. People have interpreted this parable in many different ways, but nearly everyone agrees that God wants us to show that we are trustworthy in small ways before he entrusts us with bigger responsibilities.

One of the small ways that I can be a good steward of God's gifts is by making investments that reflect my values. I have my brother to thank for introducing me to ethically motivated (also called "socially responsible") investing—an investment strategy that seeks to maximize both financial return and social good. Richard, a Wharton School of Business graduate, opened a socially responsible investment fund when our first child was born. Over the years, we used that fund to save for Clark's and Emma's education. It felt good to know that the money we were investing reflected our values.

In the last decade, more and more socially responsible funds have opened. Some target specific issues, such as inhumane working conditions or respect for God's creation, but most group together a number of corporate responsibility issues. With a little research or the help of a knowledgeable financial adviser, you can find options that align with your values while providing the return and level of risk that fit your investment profile.

Though Richard, who died when our children were still in grade school, did not live long enough to see his nephew and niece use that education fund, he did leave a legacy. Richard taught me that we should invest our money to do good.

In our experience, more often than not, doing good has also meant doing well. But even if Matthew and I have not always maximized a return on an investment, we are content. As the Amish will attest, some portfolios cannot be measured solely in dollars and cents.

Let's Sum It Up

Amish attitudes toward money are based on biblical principles. Saving is encouraged; frivolous spending and coveting are not. The Amish stay out of debt, give generously, and make investments in keeping with their values. Amish businesses thrive when others fail because the goal is to make a living, not make a killing.

Think about where the US economy would be today if we applied Almost Amish principles to personal, corporate, and governmental finances. We would not spend money we did not have. We would restrain our tendencies toward greed. We would plan for the future, sacrificing immediate gratification for the long-term good. We might not have the mercurial highs, but we also would avoid the devastating crashes that have left so many homeless and hopeless in recent years. We would take care of the poor among us. Those with more would help those with less.

In the spirit of delayed gratification, I have saved the best, and perhaps best-known, biblically based financial advice for last: "Store your treasures in heaven, where moths and rust cannot destroy, and thieves do not break in and steal. Wherever your treasure is, there the desires of your heart will also be" (Matthew 6:20-21). From God's lips to our ears. Amen and Amen!

CHAPTER 4

NATURE

Time spent in God's creation reveals the face of God.

IT ALL STARTED IN A GARDEN, as so many good things do.

Shortly after we moved to Kentucky, a new friend, Sharon, invited me to her house. Sharon lives in an economically challenged section of town alongside people of various racial and ethnic backgrounds, including refugee families. Since we are both social exercisers, we decided to go for a walk. Two blocks from her house, Sharon stopped in front of a large empty lot wedged between the fire station and an old cemetery. The lot was filled with trash and broken bottles and had a well-deserved reputation as Drug Deal Central.

"Can't you just see it? This is the perfect place for a community garden."

Even at three in the afternoon, I did not feel comfortable

entering the abandoned lot, so I was grateful that Sharon stayed on the sidewalk while she shared her vision. "I've already talked to the church that owns the land, and they've given me the tentative green light. The fire department says it will provide water. And since firefighters are coming and going around the clock, their presence will help prevent vandalism."

In truth, I could not "see it," but Sharon was so enthusiastic I tried to stay positive. "That cemetery is beautiful. What's the history of this place?"

"Thanks for asking." (I later learned that this is one of Sharon's trademark responses, and it never fails to bring me joy.) "I've been doing some research. Here's the short version: in the 1840s, there was a terrible cholera epidemic throughout Lexington. A saint of a man, London Ferrell, was an African American pastor in the area. He and the white pastor of the Episcopal church here went around visiting the sick and burying the dead together. Long after the epidemic passed, London Ferrell died and the city held a huge parade honoring him. He was the only African American ever allowed to be buried in this cemetery."

When she gets going, Sharon's eyes remind me of sparklers on the Fourth of July. This was shaping up to be more than the normal community garden. I was intrigued.

"How did you get the church interested in the garden project?"

"The elders have been looking for a way to show restitution to this now predominantly African American neighborhood. They see the community garden as an opportunity to bring about racial reconciliation, with people of all ethnic backgrounds working side by side in what is essentially a food desert."

Ever the pragmatic, I asked, "Okay, I'm sold. What do we need to make it happen?"

"Volunteers, funding, and a whole lot of prayer. We'll have to build a fence across the front, for security. And I'd like to plant a demonstration orchard with fruit and nut trees. It would be great if we could bring in a local artist to involve school kids in making colorful signs . . ."

God must have a thing for gardens. Within weeks of this conversation, a grant opportunity appeared in my in-box. Sharon's vision and this funder were truly a match made in heaven. The dream became a reality.

Gardeners have a saying: the first year a seedling sleeps, the second year it creeps, and the third year it leaps. My, how this garden has leaped! With several dozen individual plots, a large community garden to provide fresh produce for a local homeless shelter and an after-school program, a meditation space and labyrinth with perennial flower gardens, and a demonstration orchard, the London Ferrell Community Garden is thriving. The project continues to expand with cooking classes, experiential education in the local schools, and composting partnerships with local businesses.

Last Christmas, when Matthew and I downsized to our town house, the hardest thing for me to give up was my garden. Solution: contact the London Ferrell garden and sign up for a plot—just a short bike ride from our new home.

One early morning in June, I was watering and weeding in the garden. Thanks to the community compost bins and a mountain of aged manure, my vegetables were growing like gangbusters—which this garden has literally done (bust up drug gangs). I worked alone until an elderly woman arrived with her dog. The woman showed me around her plot. The tomatoes and peppers looked healthy, though a bit thirsty, so I offered to drag the hose over. We chatted for a bit, and then I asked if she could use some extra produce—we could barely keep up with our lettuce and peas. She gladly accepted a bundle, and I gratefully accepted her smile. What a perfect way to start my day, working in the garden with a new friend, as God intended.

A Bit of Amish History

Appreciation of nature is a core Christian value, and central to the Amish way of life. If we love the Creator, we should also love his creation. Living off the land serves as a daily reminder that everything we have depends on God.

Because of persecution in the Old World, the Amish fled from Switzerland to isolated regions where they taught themselves farming skills as a means of survival. When they came to North America, they sought and settled in rural areas with rich farmland.

For the Amish, God is manifested in the soil, the weather, the plants, and the animals that surround them. One of humanity's highest callings is the care of this creation. The first chapter of Genesis repeatedly states that God believes his creation is "good." One way we show our love for God is by loving what he loves. If God loves his creation, so should we.

Another key way the Amish show their love for God is through obedience. One of the first instructions in the Bible is for man to tend and protect the garden—*abad* and *shamar* in Hebrew. This is not a suggestion; it's a command. As the Old Testament repeatedly demonstrates, bad things happen when we disobey God. Stewardship of the land is a tangible way for us to demonstrate our love for the Creator.

The Amish also understand that the earth does not belong to us; rather, it is on loan from God. Psalm 24:1 teaches us that "The earth is the LORD's, and everything in it." If we borrowed a horse and buggy from God, we would not want to return it with the mare unfed, dehydrated, and lame or the buggy full of beer bottles and cigarette butts.

While fewer Amish make their living entirely on the farm, nearly all live in rural areas and supplement their income with gardens and livestock. Feeding a horse is a far different activity than is feeding the gas tank of a car; cars and horses get us where we want to go, but the lessons we learn from birthing, grooming, feeding, mucking, and loving another of God's creatures cannot be gained in driver's ed.

Knowing God through Nature

The Amish are not the first to see earth stewardship as a Christian responsibility. From the beginning of church history, sages have told us we need to spend time in nature in order to see the face of God. The Amish, by sticking to a traditional way of life, have resisted the trends that these sages warned against. Here is a sampling of what some fathers of the faith have taught:

> The initial step for a soul to come to knowledge of God is contemplation of nature.
> IRENAEUS (CA. 120–CA. 202)

> Nature is schoolmistress, the soul the pupil; and whatever one has taught or the other has learned has come from God—the Teacher of the teacher.
> TERTULLIAN (160–CA.230), *De Testimonio Animae*

> I want creation to penetrate you with so much admiration that wherever you go, the least plant may bring you the clear remembrance of the Creator.
> BASIL THE GREAT (329–379), *Hexaemeron*, HOMILY V, "THE GERMINATION OF THE EARTH"

> Some people, in order to discover God, read books. But there is a great book: the very appearance of created things. Look above you! Look below you! Read it. God, whom you want to discover, never wrote that book with ink. Instead He set before your eyes the things that He had made. Can you ask for a louder voice than that?
> ST. AUGUSTINE (354–430), *De Civit. Dei*, BOOK XVI

The whole earth is a living icon of the face of God.

ST. JOHN OF DAMASCUS (675–749), TREATISE

Christ wears "two shoes" in the world: Scripture and nature. Both are necessary to understand the Lord, and at no stage can creation be seen as a separation of things from God.

JOHN SCOTTUS ERIUGENA (810–877)

I see You in the field of stars
I see You in the yield of the land
In every breath and sound, a blade of grass, a simple flower,
An echo of Your holy Name.

ABRAHAM IBN EZRA (1092–1167)

In more modern terms, George Washington Carver captures the wisdom of these church fathers as follows: "I love to think of nature as an unlimited broadcasting station through which God speaks to us every hour, if we will only tune in."

Love of Nature versus Love of Technology

Of course, spiritual writers are not the only ones to hold the natural world in high esteem. Many twenty-first-century biologists and social scientists are warning that our attraction to technology is separating us from nature. Here's how I summarize their arguments: gardens grow vegetables; technology turns us into vegetables.

E. O. Wilson is a biologist at Harvard who believes that human beings have an innate attraction to nature. He calls this attraction *biophilia*. Oliver R. W. Pergams and Patricia A. Zaradic are two researchers who came up with a related word, *videophilia*. They use this term to describe our attraction to electronic media.

Pergams and Zaradic contend that our tendency to focus on sedentary activities involving electronic media is separating us from nature. We are spending less time in parks, less time camping and hiking, and less time in unstructured outdoor play because videophilia is replacing biophilia.

This research certainly seems to be borne out in daily observations, doesn't it? Yet as valid as these premises are, they do not go far enough. They speak amply of the natural component, but they fail to take into account the spiritual one.

We do have an innate love of nature (biophilia): God loves his creation, and we love what God loves because he made us in his image. But there is ample evidence that green time is being replaced by screen time (videophilia). Four minutes of unstructured play outdoors versus more than six hours of screen time each day certainly does have a profound effect on our children—physically, mentally, and emotionally.

And what these researchers are not addressing is the spiritual illiteracy that results. Unlike the Amish, who are still connected to the outdoors, the rest of us are forgetting the language of God's creation.

Gifts from the Garden

While relaxing on a friend's back porch over a spicy vegetarian stew and homemade bread, the conversation turned, naturally, to food. Everyone around the table expressed concern over how much junk food kids eat and how little time children spend outdoors. Our host said that she watches every afternoon as a group of elementary schoolchildren head to the corner market to purchase their after-school snack. Each child comes out with a supersized soda and a bag of potato chips. Not a small bag—the family size, for each child, every day.

A recent study published in the *New England Journal of Medicine* tracking more than 120,000 people for a period of up to two decades identified potato-chip consumption as the number one culprit in weight gain. Two-thirds of American adults are now obese or overweight. Childhood obesity has tripled in the last three decades. If these children were harvesting potatoes after school instead of potato chips, their health would benefit.

I doubt that many of these schoolchildren connect the puffy fried wafers that come out of a cellophane bag with the spuds we buy from the produce section. Even fewer know that potatoes grow underground. With no backyard garden, would they recognize potato "eyes"? Have they seen white potato flowers swaying in a summer breeze? Do they know that the visible part needs to die before full maturation takes place— just as parts of us need to die before we can grow in Christ?

These latchkey kids—as well as the average urban or

suburban child—have never experienced the miracle of watching one seed potato produce a handful of Yukon Gold. They do not know the joy of unearthing a dozen small "new" potatoes for dinner. They have never experienced the springtime joy of stumbling upon stray potatoes that escaped last fall's harvest.

Oh, if every church and school had a garden, how different this world might be! Caring for a garden provides something that cannot be purchased at the grocery store: the satisfaction of eating food planted, tended, and harvested with our own hands. A garden cultivates gratitude, reminding us that every ounce of food that passes our lips ultimately comes from God. And as any experienced gardener will attest, a garden keeps us humble—constantly aware that the enemy, entropy, is very much alive.

Since the beginning of time, God has been teaching humans in the garden. I am no master gardener, but here are a few lessons I've managed to glean:

1. Satan lives in the garden. His name is Cutworm.
2. There are good bugs and bad bugs. Wisdom comes in knowing the difference.
3. Good bugs eat bad bugs. But some good bugs, such as the praying (and preying!) mantis, also eat good bugs. That's why God invented entomologists.
4. Planting and harvesting are exciting. Weeding and watering are not.
5. Three zucchini hills are two too many.

6. If we could invent a way to run power plants using overgrown zucchini, our energy woes would be over.
7. Humus is good for the garden. Hubris is not.
8. Tomatoes warm from the vine taste (at least) as good as candy.
9. Children who do not like vegetables will eat sugar peas from the shell.
10. When Mary mistook Jesus for the gardener, it was no mistake: Jesus is the new Adam, and the garden is God's eternal classroom.

The Almost Amish Way: Spend Time in Nature

There is so much to be learned by choosing to spend more of life outdoors. In twenty-first-century terms, nature is tweeting and text messaging communications from God constantly, but we are too busy to tune in. Here are some ways we can block out distractions and abide with God in his natural world:

Grow a garden

I have a friend who is a master gardener. She believes that nearly every spiritual lesson can be taught by a garden. I agree, especially if those lessons are accompanied by fresh raspberries eaten straight from the bush.

Some first steps: If you have never had a vegetable garden before, start small. Even a ten-by-ten space can grow a lot of produce, especially if you train your vines to grow vertically.

If you do not have access to a yard, start with patio planters or investigate community gardens. Another option: join a CSA (community-supported agriculture) and barter labor for part of your "share."

Begin with vegetables you know your family likes—if they don't like beets or radishes, don't bother, even though they are easy to grow. When you get more experienced, you can try introducing some fun varieties, such as blue potatoes or sun-loving tomatillos, which mature in a paper-like husk. And don't forget the herbs: they are simple to grow, don't take up much space, and add color and flavor to almost every meal.

Pack a picnic

Picnics can make an ordinary meal anything but routine. Matthew and I picnicked on some of our first dates, and we've continued to dine alfresco regularly for three decades. Most meals have been simple but romantic—a blanket spread in the backyard makes even PLT (pickle, lettuce, and tomato) sandwiches taste special. I try to pack picnic meals when we're on the road as a cheaper, healthier alternative to fast food. We've picnicked at the beach, in the woods, in fields, in cemeteries, at rest stops, in parks, and on playgrounds.

For our thirtieth anniversary, we packed up homemade crab cakes (thanks to my mother) and ate them on the grounds of a local estate. The historic buildings are closed in the evening, but the grounds are left open. We had the gardens to ourselves—with extra ambience supplied by friendly fireflies.

Since moving to downtown Lexington, we have been picnicking more than ever. Within easy walking distance we've discovered three parks with picnic tables. The park closest to us also has a gazebo, where we've enjoyed watermelon after our family Friday night dinners.

In addition, we've found that picnics make for easy entertaining. A couple of weeks ago, we picnicked with friends and their three small children in the park behind our house. The kids played on the equipment while the grown-ups talked. My friend made a warm pasta and pesto salad, and I brought cheese, fruit, and carrot cake to round out the meal. Bonus: no clean-up. The birds ate all the crumbs.

Picnics create a memorable oasis—a time set apart from everyday life—to be in nature and to enjoy God's sustaining gifts. What could be more holy than saying grace and breaking bread together in the shade of a life-giving tree?

Pick up trash

Last Saturday, Matthew and I went for an early morning walk. We were pleasantly surprised when our son, Clark, and his wife, Val, approached us from behind. They had spied us leaving our courtyard and hurried to catch up with us. We wandered back to their place, through a hedgerow and a flat meadow near the university. Clark pointed to a mess of soda cans and discarded fast-food bags: "I just cleaned up this pathway a few weeks ago. Guess it's time to come back out with some trash bags."

My mother's heart swelled. Clark has received many awards in college and medical school, but this humble act gave me more joy than all his academic accolades put together. Why? Because it showed he has a servant's heart. He was obeying the command to tend and care for the garden (Genesis 2:15) while showing his love for God and for his neighbors, with no expectation of thanks or recognition.

Often on our morning walk through the park, I bring two bags—one for trash and one for recycling. The park is well used by little kids on swings, skateboarders with tattoos, basketball players in high-tops, and baseball teams young and old. One afternoon, we saw college students string a cord a few feet off the ground between two trees and try tightrope walking—far harder than it looks in the movies. A few days later, we watched a young man impressing his date—and us—by juggling bowling pins. With dozens of countries and ethnic groups represented, the park is a regular United Nations.

The garden aspires to Eden, yet is marred by litter. Each morning, we are presented with new opportunities to pick up cans and bottles. Yes, our hands get dirty, and once I even negligently cut my finger on a broken bottle. But these are minuscule prices to pay for the joy of participating in God's restoration.

Survey your neighborhood. Do you have a ravine where old items have been dumped for years? A favorite teen hangout that gets trashed every Saturday night? A street (maybe your own) with garbage along the shoulders? Anyone can help clean up public spaces.

Get in the habit of carrying a bag when you go on a walk and picking up trash along the way. Gather a bunch of kids from your church, school, or neighborhood to clean up a streambed. Ask your church or school to adopt a highway. Work with your neighborhood association to be sure there are trash and recycling barrels in convenient locations. Plant and tend a flower garden at a busy intersection. Make it a goal to leave every place you live more beautiful than when you arrived.

Plant a tree

One of the best investments you can make in the future is to plant a tree.

I grew up Jewish, in a tradition that values tree planting. Here's a story from the Talmud, the central text of mainstream Judaism:

> While the sage, Honi, was walking along a road, he saw a man planting a carob tree. Honi asked him, "How long will it take for this tree to bear fruit?"
>
> "Seventy years," replied the man.
>
> Honi then asked, "Are you so healthy a man that you expect to live that length of time and eat its fruit?"
>
> The man answered, "I found a fruitful world

because my ancestors planted it for me. Likewise
I am planting for my children." (*Taanit 23a*, third
century or before)

A couple of centuries later, the rabbis concurred: "Even if
you are old, you must plant. Just as you found trees planted
by others, you must plant them for your children" (*Midrash
Tanchuma, Kodashim 8*, fourth to fifth centuries).

When I was growing up, we commemorated special occasions by planting a tree in Israel. Deaths, births, anniversaries,
marriages, bar mitzvahs—all were occasions for planting a
tree. Send in a donation to the tree-planting Jewish National
Fund in honor of Grandma's birthday or Johnny's graduation, and you will receive a beautiful certificate.

Lots of small saplings add up. When the state of Israel was
formed in 1948, it was a barren land. Now, lush belts of green
cover 250,000 acres, providing green lungs around congested
cities and recreation and respite for all Israelis. Trees indig-
enous to the Middle East such as native oaks, carob, redbud,
almond, pear, hawthorn, cypress, and Atlantic cedar have
brought the desert back to life.

We can do the same here. If you take a walk in many well-
off neighborhoods, you'll notice that the streets are tree lined.
Go to the poor sections of town, and they are barren. Trees give
shade, increase home values, reduce crime, clean the air, add
beauty, and glorify God. Just as the Jewish National Fund has
planted 240 million trees in the barren land of Israel, churches
can plant "trees of life" throughout blighted urban areas of

the United States. (Shameless plug: If you want to help, visit www.blessedearth.org/treeplanting.) And poor areas are not the only areas that need trees. When a church plants trees in towns devastated by tornadoes, floods, and other weather-related disasters, they are also planting hope.

Too often, Christians are known for what we are *against*. Tree planting offers a wholesome opportunity to be known by what we are *for*.

Work outdoors

Many of us parents are afraid to give our kids chores. Because both parents work or parents are divorced or there never were two parents in the picture, we feel guilty. So, instead of following scriptural principles that warn against spoiling children, we coddle them. But coddling is copping out. It circumvents the hard work of parenting. In our desire to sidestep sulking or hissy fits, we sedate kids with digital distractions.

What we forget is that *giving* kids chores is exactly that: a gift. Does Junior really need to know how to rake leaves? Perhaps not, but raking leaves will teach him important lessons about staying on task, teamwork, and delayed satisfaction. Watering the garden encourages responsibility: if plants get too dry, they die. Mowing the lawn requires that safety procedures are followed; sticks and stones can break bones (or at least the lawn mower's "bones") if not picked up *before* mowing.

Teaching children the satisfaction of a job well done is a positive feedback loop. The more skills they develop, the more confidence they have. Greater confidence leads to more complex jobs, which expand their proficiencies even further.

For better and for worse, children learn from our example. If we believe that outdoor work is beneath us, they will too. If we see it as a time to be with God while enjoying sunshine and fresh air, they will too. Inviting our children or a friend to work alongside us allows us to experience companionship and learn from each other. In order to see, hear, smell, taste, and touch God's creation, we need to work alongside him.

From an early age, Amish children are assigned outdoor chores. These responsibilities grow along with competencies. If you live in a rural area, as most Amish do, there will always be plenty of outdoor work—either on your land or a neighbor's. If you live in a suburban setting, ask young children to help pick up twigs, sweep the walk, water plants, and spread mulch. As the children get older, they can mow grass, shovel driveways, and weed beds for you and for elderly neighbors.

In urban areas, you can clean up a playground, start a children's garden at the library, or begin a healthy soil for healthy food program. The goal is the same: to spend more time outdoors, so people can know the Creator through his creation.

Play outdoors

Physical work is necessary to keep us healthy in mind, body, and spirit. My husband prescribes an hour of physical work a day and a day of rest a week (Sabbath). But how do we get an hour of physical activity outdoors when machines and minimum-wage workers perform much of our labor?

Outdoor play is one solution. By "play" I do not necessarily mean organized sports. I mean taking a walk around the neighborhood, climbing a tree, riding bikes, running around the playground, jumping on the rope swing, digging for archaeological treasures in the creek bed, picking dandelion bouquets, playing in the leaves, making fairy houses, constructing drip castles in the sand, building snow forts, ice-skating on the pond, flying kites. The possibilities are as big as all outdoors *if* we do not zap our imaginations with digital addictions.

One deterrent to outdoor play is fear. Many parents, and their children, believe it is unsafe to play outside. I'm not advising parents to be foolish: you know your neighborhood and how safe or unsafe it is. But before ruling out fresh-air play altogether, we should consider whether we are succumbing to a proven danger—diabetes, heart disease, and obesity, which come with a sedentary lifestyle— because of exaggerated fears fueled by media sensationalism. For example, it is certainly a sad truth that children are abducted in our country, and since we bear the responsibility for our children both morally and legally, we do need to be careful. But it is also a sad truth that kidnapping stories sell magazines, plain and simple.

In a Mayo Clinic study, nearly three-quarters of the parents worried that their children might be abducted. One-third of the parents said this was a frequent worry and that they worried more about kidnapping than any other concern, including car accidents, sports injuries, and drug addiction.

Abductions by strangers are rare in the United States; the chances are about .000001 to 1 that your child will be involved in a kidnapping by a stranger. The chances of your child dying in a car accident are sixty times greater, and yet we do not banish our children from automobiles.

If you are concerned about safety, be choosy about location. But set a goal that you and your children will spend at least an hour each day outdoors. It will change your physical, emotional, and mental health. It will change your relationship with God. With practice, it can shift your focus from "all about me" to "all about we."

Let's Sum It Up

Sometimes when Matthew is giving a talk, he pauses and asks folks to buddy up for a few minutes and discuss how God speaks to them. We've heard a wide range of answers: God speaks through Scripture, through events in our lives, through people we encounter, through dreams and visions, and in dozens of other ways. But one of the most frequent *places* where God speaks to us is in nature.

I like to call these "Romans 1:20 moments." In this verse Paul says, essentially, that we are without excuse for not knowing God if we simply take a stroll in our backyard. Romans 1:20 moments are when we stand on a beach watching the sun go down, or climb a mountain, or sit beside a stream; in the stillness, we hear God's voice. Many of the pastors we work with say they heard God's call not in a church, but in his other cathedral—in nature. Such exchanges are biblically based. As my husband likes to say, "Jesus mostly taught on field trips."

Once again, we can take a cue here from the Amish, who make the outdoors a central focus of life. The more time they spend in God's creation, the more they come to know the Creator. But the opposite is also true. The less time we spend outdoors, the more alienated from God we can become.

Scripture tells us to live in the world, not of the world. The Almost Amish extension might be to live less in the man-made world and more in the God-made world. Adjusting the ratio can be the difference between a paradise imperiled and paradise restored—an abandoned lot or a community garden. The choice is ours. The time is now.

CHAPTER 5

SIMPLICITY

Small and local leads to saner lives.

In Hollywood, it's the Oscar. In television, it's the Emmy. In journalism, it's the Pulitzer. It seems like every creative endeavor sees fit to give out a pinnacle award. When I was asked to write the introduction to the thirtieth anniversary edition of the Mennonite classic *Living More with Less*, I felt as if I had been awarded the Nobel Prize for Simple Living. Talk about irony: the Mennonites are the living lightly experts, not me.

For years, I've been using the *More with Less Cookbook*, the beloved companion to *Living More with Less*. The Mennonites are good cooks, but the book is not just about food; it's about a way of life.

The Mennonites, one of those groups that go back to the same Anabaptist roots as the Amish, value simplicity just as the Amish do. Less obviously distinguishable than the Amish, many Mennonites dress in regular—though not flashy—clothes, drive cars, and work normal jobs. The one quality that universally sets both the Amish and Mennonites apart from the world is their holistic approach to simplicity.

What does a holistic approach to simplicity involve? Decluttering your home is a great starting point, but it's also about building a less complicated life. It's about supporting local farms and businesses, getting to know your neighbors, and building a relational faith community. Keeping things small and local leads to a saner life.

What I like most about this approach to simplicity is how it shines a light on the human side of Jesus, for this is what simple living is all about: God made flesh—cooking, shopping, eating, walking, talking, working, and fellowshiping on *this earth*. It's about God coming into our homes, businesses, schools, neighborhoods, and churches to show us how to live.

Two Kinds of Clutter

Simplicity involves cutting back on two major kinds of stuff—the kind that fills our houses and the kind that fills our calendars. Both, of course, are related. The more things we have, the more time we have to spend shopping, paying for, transporting, storing, caring for, and disposing of them. The Amish avoid both kinds of clutter. They don't fill their houses with lots of unnecessary things, and they don't fill their calendars running around from activity to activity.

In chapter 1, we discussed decluttering our homes. Here, we will focus on decluttering our lives. One way to do that is to aim for small and local—keeping our daily interactions within horse-and-buggy distance. Supporting small farms, patronizing small businesses, volunteering in local schools, getting to know our neighbors, and building a small faith community make our lives more simple and sane.

The world is based on the false promise of infinite growth. Amish society is based on the sustainable truth of an infinite God. The path from a crazy-busy life to a saner and simpler life begins in knowing the difference.

Amish Principles

"Less is more" is a basic principle of Amish simplicity. The Amish have not bought into the modern myth that bigger is better and faster is first. Instead, they intentionally hold their farms, businesses, schools, friendships, and faith communities to a human scale. Contentment and simplicity are two sides of the same coin. The Amish do not complicate their lives unnecessarily in the insatiable quest for more; keeping things small and local contributes to Amish peace.

Amish farming communities have a long tradition of small farms, carefully managed, with diversified crops. They farm to provide for their families, not to get rich. A homestead with a few well-tended cows, chickens, pigs, and horses along with a variety of vegetables in the garden and fruit trees in the orchard will feed a family without incurring debt, purchasing a lot of expensive machinery, or depleting the topsoil of nutrients.

In a similar way, cottage industries succeed because the Amish are not out to "make a killing." Typical Amish businesses include making high-quality wooden furniture, quilts, and specialty foods. The Amish run small restaurants, make leather saddles, and engage in many of the traditional—and nearly lost—arts. These mostly family-owned businesses are based on excellent workmanship, fulfilling real needs within the community. Fair wages for a fair day's work—not climbing the corporate ladder—is the measure of success. Doing it God's way, not doing it my way, is the Amish mission statement.

Consolidated schools, where many smaller schools are closed and a new "bigger and better" one is built, have become the norm in rural communities. Not so for the Amish. They have resisted this trend, arguing that spending an hour or more on a bus each day and navigating centralized bureaucracies is not in their children's best interests. A local school, where students of different ages learn to interact and teachers know the families, can provide a healthier learning environment. Most important, the Amish emphasize other kinds of education as well, including learning that goes on outside the classroom.

This learning takes place in the context of the community. When neighbors know neighbors, they can share skills, knowledge, and resources. The Amish love to visit, and they welcome opportunities to help one another. Knowing every family in the community makes life less complicated and overwhelming. When problems arise, they know who can help.

The church community succeeds for related reasons. You have never heard of an Amish megachurch, and you never will. The typical Amish faith community consists of thirty to forty families. Once a community gets much bigger, members will no longer know one another by name or understand how best to serve others. Rules of life are determined face-to-face by the church district, intentionally kept within the geographic proximity of horse-and-buggy transportation.

By keeping things small, the Amish have avoided some of the potential pitfalls of big farming (bankruptcy), big business (layoffs), big schools (anxiety), big cities (alienation), and big churches (isolation). In the upside-down world of Christ, less is more, the last shall come first, and the meek shall inherit the earth.

The Almost Amish Way

One way we can simplify life is to keep it small and local. By supporting small businesses, farms, schools, neighborhoods, and faith communities, we build local relationships while simplifying our lives. Below are some practical ways to discover that good things do, indeed, come in small packages.

Support local farms

A few years back, Matthew served as the visiting scholar at a college in upstate New York. Like many Christian colleges, it was built "at the end of the road" in a very rural community. This particular community includes some Amish farms as well as non-Amish ("English") ones. Throughout the surrounding countryside, we could not help but notice that most of the farms with power lines running to them are in decline: rusted tractors up on blocks, barns with roofs caving in, and "for sale" signs planted in the fields. In contrast, the farms with no power lines running to the farmhouse—the Amish farms—are neat, clean, and thriving.

Why are these Amish farms alive and well long after the family farm has been declared dead? Staying small and local is their winning formula. Supporting small, local farms can be your winning formula too: you eat healthier, your community stays prettier, and you make God smile.

How so? Let's start with health, the first bonus. That old adage, you are what you eat, is truer than ever. We live in a sea of chemicals. Many of these chemicals are hard to avoid—in the particulate matter we breathe, in the neighbor's dandelion-free grass our kids and pets play in, and in the newly carpeted classroom at school. We can, however, choose which foods to purchase and feed to our families.

I was married to Matthew throughout his decade of premed, medical school, and residency training. I am now going through the process a second time with our son and his friends. As you can imagine, the talk at the dinner table often turns to medical topics. Most of these discussions are far too technical for me to fully understand, but over the years I've picked up a few gems about lifestyle medicine, things all of us can do to improve our health.

Here's one simple piece of advice I've gleaned: *If you cannot pronounce it, don't eat it.*

Look at the list of ingredients in the snacks in your cupboard and microwavable meals in the freezer. Many of the names are so long even I, an English teacher, cannot pronounce them. For the most part, these foreign-sounding chemicals are not good for our health.

The average piece of food travels fifteen hundred miles to reach our plates. With a little extra effort, I can find food produced within fifty miles of my home—jams, maple syrup, honey, apple cider, cheese, beef, chicken, eggs, flour, rolls, bread, and a huge range of in-season fruits and vegetables. When I look at the labels on these items, the ingredients are simple and familiar. Local almost always means fewer chemicals and preservatives, which results in better nutrition for my family. It also means that fruits and vegetables do not have to be genetically modified to survive long-distance shipping.

The second bonus of family farms is lovely scenery— a place for the eye to rest. The area where Matthew and I grew up was one of the largest dairy producers in the United States. Now, there is only one dairy farm left in the entire county. The field behind my childhood home where I picked wildflower bouquets and chased fireflies is planted with tract houses. When Matthew and I went back to visit his old stomping grounds, it was like a scene out of a movie: a sign with a stone facade announcing "Woodfield Estates" and big bulldozers tearing down a barn. Ironically, of course, both the woods and the fields referred to on the sign are being destroyed.

For many suburban and urban kids, seasonal visits to a pumpkin patch, corn maze, apple orchard, or strawberry field are the only agricultural experiences they may ever have. These small farms are worth protecting. They are worth supporting. Without them our children would lose any understanding of where their food comes from. It's much harder to see the sustaining hand of God in the cereal aisle than in waves of wheat undulating in the breeze.

Which leads me to the final and most important bonus of supporting local farms. It makes God happy. How do I know? Because from Genesis to Revelation, the Bible is filled with praise for God's creation, delight in the beauty of creation, and the mandate for us to be good stewards of the garden—this earth.

The Amish understand that

- God loves creation. ("It is good," Genesis 1.)
- He owns creation. ("The earth is the LORD's," Psalm 24.)
- He entrusts its care to us. (To tend and protect the garden, Genesis 2:15)

By loving what God loves, respecting what he owns, and obeying what he commands, we please God.

Supporting the local farmers' market, buying from vegetable stands, visiting the local orchard, and shopping for local foods in the grocery aisles are simple ways we can please our Father.

Support local businesses

Once while traveling to a speaking engagement in Tennessee, Matthew and I stopped at a gas station/fast food chain/rest stop. Walking in front of us were a traditionally dressed Mennonite woman and her daughter. They looked refreshingly out of place.

For the most part, however, I rarely spot traditional Mennonite or Amish folks in chain stores. The reason is that they believe in supporting neighbors who run local businesses rather than giving their money to impersonal corporations.

For a long time, I resisted shopping locally. *Can one person really make a difference? It's easier to get everything in one store. I don't have time. It costs too much—I could use that money to support a starving child in Africa.* I had all the excuses, but the truth is that's all they were—excuses for not doing what my conscience or the Holy Spirit or my Jewish guilt told me was right. The reality was that with minimal sacrifice, I could afford to shop ethically *and* support a starving child in Africa.

When Matthew and I were first married thirty years ago, he made a concerted effort to purchase items made only in the United States or other countries that supported fair labor practices. Long before buying local became hip, Matthew went out of his way to support local businesses. Even though we had little money, it was worth a few more cents to avoid buying products made under harsh working conditions. Instead of national chains with merger mentalities, he wanted to support the personal service and local relationships that keep Main Street in business.

Over the last three decades, thousands of small businesses have died because there have not been enough Matthews. But I am hopeful yet. God does not demand that we be successful; he asks us to be faithful, even (especially!) when the prospects do not look bright.

Does that mean that I never buy from chain stores? Of course not. But I try to support businesses that are in easy walking or biking distance from my home. The barber, laundry, bakery, hardware store, and restaurants we frequent are family owned. And while the local grocery and bank may be part of a bigger chain, at least we know the cashiers and the bank manager by name. They are our neighbors.

Don't allow school to run your life

As I typed this heading, I realized that "run" is just one letter off from "ruin," and that extra letter is "I." Seems silly, but it reminds me of a serious truth about how easily we can ruin something by inserting ourselves. Often the "I" in school performance is about the parents more than the children. Very early on, we parents rush in to complete the science fair experiment or get overly involved in our child's math homework, allowing the school calendar, school projects, and school priorities to control our lives. While parental hovering may seem harmless in elementary school, it can set a pattern with lifelong consequences.

Amish communities usually run their own schools, and they keep them small. In general, when given the choice, our family has chosen smaller schools over larger ones. Our children mostly attended smallish schools and colleges, with some home schooling in the middle-school years. While many people do not have a choice about school size, we do have a choice about how big of a role academic pressures will play in our children's lives.

Unless challenged, patterns tend to repeat themselves. Some of these patterns are good: I grew up in a family that expected academic excellence, and I'm glad that Matthew and I encouraged our children to be curious, lifelong learners. I'm also happy that they showed respect for their teachers by excelling in class. Most of all, we are grateful that our children are using this learning to serve the Kingdom. But the pursuit of academic excellence also can have a dark side, in which a one-size-fits-all philosophy can fail to take God's variety into account. Ideally, learning and achievement of all kinds should be valued.

A few years back, Matthew was invited to a Bruderhof community in the Catskill Mountains. Like the Amish and Mennonite, the Bruderhof are a branch of the Anabaptists. Families in this community each live in a small apartment, but meals are prepared and eaten communally and money is shared in common, much like the first-century church.

The community supports itself in large part by manufacturing and selling products that assist physically and mentally challenged children. During his visit, Matthew helped in the factory and began talking with the young man working beside him. The young man explained that he was good with his hands but had never been academically inclined. He felt thankful that in his community he did not feel pressured to go to college. On the other hand, if someone felt called, for instance, to serve the community as a physician, the elders would give their support and even pay the tuition. In the end, this amiable young man felt he had as much value as someone with an advanced degree. His prestige was not based on years of education, but rather on his contributions to the community and service to God.

While I am not advocating that we all join the Bruderhof, we can gain much from their example. I have spent most of my working life as an educator; I love teaching and I value learning. Yet when students ask for advice about higher education, I encourage them to listen to God first. If they feel called to a life that requires a degree, they should go for it. But they should not bury themselves in student debt and fritter away years of their lives just because that's what everyone else is doing. Grades and résumé buffing can all too easily become the goal, rather than lifelong learning for the glorification of God.

In seeking that balance, I like to remember the motto carved on the entrance of Asbury University, the school where I last taught: "Academic excellence and spiritual vitality."

Remembering that the second part is at least as important as the first, and embodying both, can keep academics from claiming too large a place in our lives.

Know your neighbors

What does neighborliness have to do with simplicity? A lot! If you know your neighbors, you know their needs. And they know yours. You can help one another out. You have a support system. You don't have to go it alone.

I'll give you a few examples. One of Clark's medical school friends moved a few blocks from us. Before moving in, Joel and his wife wanted to paint the house and do a few repairs. Instead of buying drop cloths, ladders, and tools, they borrowed ours. Knowing their neighbors allowed them to save time, money, and hassle.

Close-knit neighborhoods also allow for skill swapping. I have a friend who is a master gardener. I have pruned apple and pear trees, but I did not know how to prune stone-fruit trees, such as cherry, plum, and peach. My friend offered to show me, teaching me how to hollow out the middle section of the tree, to effect a wine goblet shape. In exchange, I've helped out with child care when she and her husband are in a pinch—a "favor" that gives me great pleasure, especially since her son reminds me so much of Clark when he was little.

Sometimes it's the network of neighbors that counts. We have a friend who is finishing his dissertation and needed a temporary housing situation for a few weeks within walking distance of the local seminary. Our old home would have been perfect, but we had moved. So we called a former neighbor. They have a basement apartment, which they generously offered to our friend. Simple solution. Problem solved.

The Amish are known for their neighborliness. They love to visit, and they welcome opportunities to help one another. But there's another, deeper reason. This network of support also helps simplify their lives. When you know you can count on your neighbors, life does not seem so overwhelming. Problems that seem insurmountable alone are easily resolved when neighbors act neighborly.

Build a small faith community

For the last five years, Matthew and I have traveled to churches throughout the country giving talks on faith and the environment. One of the things we have come to appreciate is the many ways that people worship God. We have seen God at work in congregations of ten to ten thousand, in home churches and megachurches, in converted barns and soaring stone cathedrals. We have heard people speak in tongues and we have sat with those who worship without speaking at all. We have seen pastors preach in full vestments and in Hawaiian shirts, with their congregations singing traditional hymns set to contemporary music and contemporary lyrics set to traditional tunes.

God built diversity into nature to give it resilience. Diversity in the church also gives it strength. It is beautiful to see the many ways Christians worship God, just as it is beautiful to see that, though we are not all born to live the Amish life, we can all find simple ways to praise him. In our travels, we have come to appreciate one common denominator: no matter how big or small a church is, it needs to act out its faith through relationships. These relationships work best in smaller settings. Small groups go by many names: home group, faith group, discipleship group, fellowship group, affinity group, covenant group, missional group, Bible study group, new life community, and so on. No matter what they are called, they serve similar purposes, providing a setting for fellowship, accountability, and service. Only when we know one another can we help one another grow in Christ.

In our son's church every time the congregation reaches more than 120 individuals, they split off. Their focus is on Christian fellowship—living life together. They share meals, share tools, share child care, and share lives. Everyone knows each other by name. Keeping the church community small—in fact, about the same size as the typical Amish church district—creates a strong sense of belonging and a concern for one another's welfare. Life seems less complicated when you live among a group of people who share your love for Christ and are ready, willing, and able to act in his stead.

Let's Sum It Up

If the Amish made bumper stickers for their buggies, the bestseller might read, "Be not conformed to this world"

(Romans 12:2, KJV). The world believes bigger is better, yet recent history has revealed the high cost of our megasized world. Big farms fail. Bank mergers collapse. Big schools become just another form of big business. In our anonymous communities, we don't know the neighbor down the street or the person sitting beside us at church. Now we are slowly relearning what the Amish have always known: that infinite growth is not only impossible but in many instances undesirable. Focusing on an infinite God, not infinite growth, frees us from so much striving and allows us to lead simpler, less burdened lives.

In a similar way, the teachings of Christ turn the world upside down. Those with the most possessions in this life may end up with the least in the next, and the little guy shall inherit the earth. The believing beggar Lazarus is in heaven, while the man who relied only on his riches is in the hot seat.

Each of us needs to be challenged by the example of Jesus made flesh and then needs to keep doing a little better every year. It's that simple, and that hard. Thinking big by supporting small. Loving globally by purchasing locally. Losing our lives in order to gain them.

Supporting small farms and businesses, restoring learning and achievement to its proper place, interacting with our neighbors, and fellowshiping within a small faith community are daily reminders of how we can start bringing heaven here on earth—leading simpler, saner lives with people we know and love, in our local communities, this very day.

CHAPTER 6

SERVICE

Service to others reduces loneliness and isolation.

BACK WHEN I WAS TEACHING at Asbury University, I shared an office with another English professor. Brian became a friend of the family, so when he invited us to go to church with him, we gladly accepted.

It was my first time worshiping at a Mennonite church. The building is, appropriately, a converted barn. About fifty or sixty people worship together, and most of the families are related.

I happened to come on a very special Sunday—the naming ceremony for two babies, Sara and Ezra. Talk about adorable! The five- and seven-month-old cousins looked like Gerber babies: O ye of little hair and lots of happiness. I have a weakness for babies, but what captivated me even more than their plump little clapping hands was how the church leader opened the service.

Nathan stood up, a grandfatherly yet somehow youthful man who looked as though he could still mend a fence or frame up a house without working up a sweat. His body was tall and erect, but his voice faltered.

"As most of you know, I've been going through some difficult times recently. After suffering a few losses, I just haven't been able to bounce back like I usually do, despite the good counsel of our pastor—my brother, Jim—and the generous prayers of so many of you."

Nathan paused, clearing his throat before continuing. "Today I want to honor two members of our congregation who have been of particular help to me. Every time I was down, they lifted me up. On my darkest days, they made me smile. They have ministered to me in countless ways, without ever expecting anything in return."

Even from the back row I could see his eyes tear up. "These two members are like family to me. In fact they are family. And they also happen to be the youngest members of our congregation."

That's when Nathan beckoned forward the parents of Sara and of Ezra—the two members he had been referring to—and began the baby-naming ceremony. He blessed the babies and all four parents, asking them to pledge to raise their children to serve God and serve their neighbors. After a prayer, he concluded by saying, "Parents, you are not alone in your responsibility. We will help you."

Nathan then asked the congregation to rise and solemnly recite together the following promise: "With love, joy, and thanksgiving—as Christ's church, and with God's help—we promise to serve, encourage, and support you as you follow Jesus and train your children in the truth."

What I loved most about this Mennonite tradition is how it underscores the reciprocal nature of service. The parents, aunts, uncles, grandparents, and great-grandparents all agreed to help serve these two helpless, precious children grow to healthy adulthood. And the babies, though too young to speak, were already ministering to the church community, as Nathan so eloquently testified. Both the giver and the receiver get something back from the act of service. The more they give, the more they gain.

This reciprocity also permeates our relationship with God. He wants us to serve him with a glad heart, not because he is lacking anything, but because the very act of getting outside our selfish, small concerns enriches *us*. Service is the agent through which we act out our love for God and for one another. Serve God: serve your neighbor. In doing one, we are doing the other.

In the beginning, God asked Adam to name the animals and then instructed humanity to serve and protect not only his creatures but all creation. Naming is both an act of intimacy and a commitment of responsibility. The Mennonite naming ceremony reminded me that all of us are being served, constantly, by God through the actions of our neighbors. It's our responsibility to acknowledge these acts, to give thanks, and to reciprocate with everyone, everywhere, every chance we get.

Serving Others

After the naming ceremony, the pastor gave a sermon on worshiping false idols. I was struck by this topic because of its juxtaposition to a strongly interdependent tradition. One of the great false idols of our day is independence. Despite (or because of) our hyperconnectedness, this independence often leads to isolation and its twin, loneliness. We live in communities where neighbors rarely catch glimpses of their next-door neighbors, let alone share one another's lives. Hundreds of miles separate family members. Jobs are transient. Marriages are until digital distractions do us part.

As with the Mennonites, daily interaction within the Amish community makes such isolation nearly impossible. When something goes wrong, the community is there to fill the gaps. If a husband falls ill, the firewood is cut by neighbors. He does not need to worry about farm chores getting done or crops being harvested—the community will pitch in. When a wife gives birth, her friends and family will help with meals, child care, and household chores. A young farmer who faces an unexpected loss will receive not only helpful advice but a loan of tools. When there is a fire, the community, not an insurance company, is there.

While Scripture tells us to do good to all people, the Amish take especially seriously Paul's admonition to care for their own "household of faith" (Galatians 6:10, kjv). Though not all Amish make their living directly on the farm, communal activities continue to bind them together. Quilting, sewing, and special days when women will gather to share household chores allow not only for many hands to make light work, but for neighbors to know the needs and circumstances of one another. Preparing a house and barn for the worship service, which takes place every two weeks, requires not only families working together, but the participation of the entire community. While barn raisings after a fire may seem like an Amish cliché, the principle is not: God reveals himself every day through the actions and words of our neighbors, if only we have eyes to see and ears to listen.

Two Kinds of Service

In general, service takes two forms: service to people we know and service to those we don't. The Amish engage in both.

Service within the community is primarily informal. Because word of mouth travels even faster than Facebook, the Amish know the needs of their neighbors and help out as a regular matter of course. There is little hesitancy to accept help and no awkward sense of obligation because the give-and-take is mutual—a normal part of Christian community.

For large disasters, they draw upon a more formal program of assistance. The Amish Aid Society was established in 1875 to spread the costs of disaster across the community. Families contribute to a general fund once every year or so, based on the value of their property. The purpose is to provide a network of support to one another. It operates without insurance agents, office buildings, copiers, computers, lawyers, or lobbyists. Lack of bureaucracy means no overhead and no seven-figure salaried executives. Because neighbors are helping neighbors, assistance always wears a human face.

The Amish also have a reputation for coming to the aid of those outside the community through their sister organization, the Mennonite Disaster Society—a network of volunteers who respond with cleanup, repair, and rebuilding assistance after tornadoes, hurricanes, floods, and other disasters. In recent years, there has been tremendous demand for relief workers. Because Mennonite and Amish people often possess higher-than-average practical skills and a strong work ethic, their services are highly valued.

Jesus as Example

Of course, it's little wonder that the Amish are so service oriented: they try to model their lives after the pattern set by Christ. It is he who is our highest example of service.

Throughout the Gospels, Jesus is constantly serving his community. Jesus, for instance, heals the mother-in-law of his disciple Peter. In one of his most dramatic miracles, he serves Lazarus, the beloved brother of Mary and Martha, by raising him from the dead. But he also serves people in his faith community who are not close friends. He helps the paralyzed walk, the blind see, and the deaf hear. He cures epilepsy, stops hemorrhaging, ends fevers, and restores a withered hand.

Though his first mission is to serve the Jewish people, Jesus also makes it his business to help strangers. "News about him spread as far as Syria, and people soon began bringing to him all who were sick. And whatever their sickness or disease, or if they were demon possessed or epileptic or paralyzed— he healed them all" (Matthew 4:24). Many of these people are non-Jews, or Gentiles. For example, in chapter 3 we discussed the story of the ten lepers. Nine of these lepers are Jews, but the one who returns to give thanks is a Samaritan, an ethnic group that, to put it mildly, did not get along well with Jesus' people. Perhaps the most famous foreigner is the Roman centurion. Jesus heals his servant because of the centurion's great faith (see Matthew 8:5-13). Jesus even travels to hostile territory, Tyre and Sidon, where he heals the demon-possessed daughter of the Canaanite woman.

The Amish follow the example of Jesus. They primarily serve those within the community where they know the needs and where opportunities abound. But, when appropriate, the Amish also travel to "foreign territory" to provide relief in times of disaster.

Helping Through Being Rather Than Doing

Remember the story of Sara and Ezra, the two babies who ministered to the congregation and to Nathan in particular?

They did not *do* anything to serve others. Their gift to the congregation was in *being* a healing presence.

The Amish certainly are doers of good. But one of their most attractive qualities—and one of the most important ways they serve the outside world—is simply by being who they are. Like Sara and Ezra, the Amish show us that a more innocent, less harried state of being is still possible. They preserve skills and practical arts that would otherwise be lost. And they demonstrate that life without communication technology is not only doable but desirable. By taking us back, they help us move forward. Teaching through example, the Amish show us how to make conscious choices about the kind of world we want to leave to Sara, Ezra, and all the other utterly dependent babies of the world.

The Almost Amish Way: Service to God and Others

The Amish look for opportunities to serve children, parents, neighbors, coworkers, and the faith community. In serving others, they are serving God. Throughout the following sections, we will look at examples of service and see how this Amish ethic can be applied in our twenty-first-century lives.

Serving children

The very first book I remember being given was *Little House in the Big Woods*, by Laura Ingalls Wilder. Laura, like the Amish today, reminds us of a time when helping Ma make piecrusts or Pa collect maple sap was a labor of love.

In second grade our daughter, Emma, lived a whole year through the eyes of Laura and her sister Mary. She dug in the banks of our creek bed, unearthing shards of pottery and beads like Laura did in *Little House on the Prairie*. She practiced sewing with her eyes shut, trying to make perfect stitches like Mary did after she went blind. And she became obsessed with cooking pancakes, like Almanzo did during *The Long Winter*. Our family cheerfully ate those first few soupy-middle batches, which Emma more than made up for later with years of breakfast-for-dinner blueberry pancakes, an enduring family favorite.

Some children, however, end up more like blind Mary than Laura, dependent on their parents even as adults. One of the most beautiful examples of parents serving children is our friends, Chris and Cara. We met Chris when he was in medical school with Matthew. Cara was pregnant with Robin while I was pregnant with Clark. At the end of her pregnancy, Cara stopped feeling Robin move, so they went to the hospital. Unfortunately, Robin had been in distress for quite a while, so the doctors performed an emergency C-section. Robin was essentially born dead. The medical team brought her back to life, but she was left permanently and severely brain damaged. Now twenty-four, Robin cannot walk or talk or care for herself, and at many times in her life, she has been unable to breathe or eat without a tube.

Because of their deep faith in Jesus, Chris and Cara took care of Robin at home. They had two "normal" children, who—like so many siblings of disabled children—have grown into extraordinary adults. Through the example set by their parents, they learned to love Robin for who she is, helping with her feeding, transport, entertainment, and bodily care with grace-filled joy.

In the most important ways, however, Chris and Cara treat Robin exactly like their other children. As parents, their job is to prepare Robin for later life, just as it is our duty to prepare children—our own and those within our spheres of influence—for adulthood.

Serving children can be frustrating and demanding and exhausting—like riding an emotional roller coaster without a safety bar. But it can also be exhilarating, fun, and delightful, teaching us to become selfless in ways that are often not otherwise possible.

Robin now resides in a group home, just a few miles from Chris and Cara. To the extent possible, Robin lives as an independent adult. Chris and Cara have prepared her for adulthood and continue to be involved in her life.

Their care for Robin mirrors God's care for us. We are helpless, hopeless, and often severely disabled without our Father's strength. Yet as the apostle Paul says, God wants to help us grow from spiritual infancy to spiritual adulthood (see 1 Corinthians 3:1-4).

The Amish expect their children to gradually learn the skills necessary to serve others. If we are to serve our children in the fullest sense, we must prepare them physically, emotionally, and spiritually for adulthood. The model set by the Amish and by our friends Chris and Cara is not the path of least resistance, but it is the path of greatest reward, ultimately, for both parent and child.

Serving parents

The Amish take care of their aging parents. It's an expected part of life—a joy, not a burden. Just as parents will build wings onto their homes for their married children, so the established children will build additions for aging parents and grandparents. One child will add an apartment onto his or her home, while the other children and grandchildren participate in the care. In this way, elders do not become isolated and can share their wisdom and experience with the younger generations, even as their own physical abilities diminish and they begin to need care again themselves.

This is a rule of living we can certainly—if not always easily—adopt as our own. One of the most beautiful examples of service to parents that I have witnessed came from a non-Amish colleague at Asbury. When this family moved to town, they purchased a home that could accommodate his mother-in-law. They built a separate apartment for her within the modest house. She lived with them for seven years. It was a win-win-win: my friends had a built-in babysitter, the grandchildren loved being able to visit Grandma, and Grandma was never lonely. She had her separate space, but she also was very much involved in the family's daily lives.

Not once by word, tone, or action did I ever detect even a hint of resentment from my colleague. When his mother-in-law was released to heaven after a difficult last illness, the family grieved, and yet even more than sorrow, they felt blessed. They had no guilt, no regrets, no lost chances to haunt them. In serving Grandma, they were ministered to; in giving, they received a trove of memories.

Again, caring for our parents echoes our relationship with God. Instead of keeping tabs on who gives what to whom, God operates out of infinite abundance.

The Amish understand that serving our earthly fathers, just like serving our heavenly Father, helps us grow as spiritual beings. In the upside-down world of Christ, we reap more than we sow and we gain more than we give.

Serving neighbors

Long, long ago, in a city far, far away, I worked for a Fortune 500 company as a director of communications. By the time Matthew was in his final year of medical school, we had been married seven years. We planned for our child to arrive at the end of April, a month before Matthew would graduate.

But our baby had other ideas. In mid-February, while celebrating my dad's birthday, I started to feel strange pains in my abdomen. I described them to Matthew. He called the doctor, who instructed Matthew to give me a glass or two of wine (an old-fashioned remedy to slow labor) and then head to the hospital. When I arrived, I was tipsy and the labor had stopped. I don't normally drink, and definitely did not during pregnancy, so the alcohol had an immediate and strong effect. The nurses pegged me as a hapless, drunk mom-to-be. Five minutes after our arrival, the alcohol wore off and the contractions started again.

My preterm labor brought an abrupt end to my seven-year career with the company, as I spent the next seven weeks on strict bed rest and never returned to the office. For a type A personality like me, Alcatraz would have been a better sentence: at least the prisoners get to do jumping jacks in the prison yard. But bed rest was also one of the most game-changing nonevents of my life. Before, I had been a giver, rarely a receiver. Bed rest left me dependent. I was forced to accept help or risk endangering the life of my unborn child.

My coworkers dropped off meals, knit bootees and blankets for the baby, and thought up creative ways to spoil me. Matthew left a plate of fruit, a pitcher of water, and books by my bed each morning, came home to fix me lunch, and cleaned the apartment meticulously so I wouldn't be tempted to get up. My mom ran errands, kept me company, and contributed meals. And my downstairs neighbor, a nurse married to a medical resident, brought their little toddler up to visit with me so I would not forget the purpose of my incarceration.

One of the angels in my life was an obstetrics nurse. I was in and out of the hospital a number of times, and somehow she ended up "adopting" me. We became friends. She called me and even visited me at home. She calmed my first-time-mother fears, lent me books, and gave me a set of cloth diaper covers that I could use once Clark was born. Her quiet, beyond-the-call-of-duty attentions lessened my anxiety and offered me peace.

By God's grace, acting through the kind hearts and actions of my circle of friends, Clark stayed put until April and emerged a healthy seven-pounder with fully developed lungs. I learned several lessons while on bed rest:

1. Tipsy pregnant women are not looked upon kindly in the OB ward.
2. Once you are sober, OB nurses will cover you with warm blankets and tender care.
3. In heaven, I'm pretty sure angels will greet us with warm blankets.
4. Even the best laid plans can change in an instant.
5. When life takes a bad turn, friends can help—but only if you let them.
6. It is often harder to receive than to give.
7. Dependency is humbling, but good for the soul.
8. Coming to a complete stop can change everything, including career ambitions.
9. Sometimes it takes a village to bear a baby.
10. Every child's first cry is a miracle from God, the Great Deliverer.

Such an upswelling of care for a woman on bed rest is a reminder that we don't have to be Amish—just Almost Amish—to serve and be served. In the Amish world, this response would be the norm; in my world, I had never before witnessed anything like it. In particular, the care I received from my colleagues, mostly secretaries and clerks twice my age, was nothing short of miraculous. Many lived as far as sixty miles away from me, and yet they still acted as my neighbors.

Clark is the evidence of their grace. It saved his life, and changed mine. I am forever grateful.

Serving God

After the naming ceremony at the Mennonite service, the pastor preached on the false idols that we continue to worship in the twenty-first century. Anything we withhold from God, he said, can become an idol. The pastor then read from 1 Samuel 1:9-11, where the childless Hannah has been despairing for a long period about her infertility:

> Once after a sacrificial meal at Shiloh, Hannah got
> up and went to pray. Eli the priest was sitting at his
> customary place beside the entrance of the Tabernacle.
> Hannah was in deep anguish, crying bitterly as
> she prayed to the LORD. And she made this vow:
> "O LORD of Heaven's Armies, if you will look upon
> my sorrow and answer my prayer and give me a son,
> then I will give him back to you. He will be yours
> for his entire lifetime, and as a sign that he has been
> dedicated to the LORD, his hair will never be cut."

In response, Eli the priest reprimands Hannah for being drunk.

Seeing her lips moving but hearing no sound, he thought she had been drinking. "Must you come here drunk?" he demanded. "Throw away your wine!"

"Oh no, sir!" she replied. "I haven't been drinking wine or anything stronger. But I am very discouraged, and I was pouring out my heart to the LORD. Don't think I am a wicked woman! For I have been praying out of great anguish and sorrow."

"In that case," Eli said, "go in peace! May the God of Israel grant the request you have asked of him."

"Oh, thank you, sir!" she exclaimed. Then she went back and began to eat again, and she was no longer sad.

I SAMUEL 1:13-18

Of all the women in the Bible, I think I identify most with Hannah—and not just because both of us were once mistakenly chastised for being inebriated! Like Hannah, I waited a long time (through seven years of Matthew's schooling) before bearing my first child. Like Hannah, becoming a mother was not an easy path—Hannah's infertility led to taunting, my early labor led to bed rest. And like Hannah, I was overcome with gratitude upon the birth of my son, though my first response ("He's perfect!") was not nearly as eloquent as Hannah's prayer of praise, the Magnificat of the Old Testament (see 1 Samuel 2:1-10).

There is also a dark side, which Hannah and I share. It could be easy to twist a good thing, such as motherhood, into an idol. In a few years, it will not be easy for me to "lose" Clark, when he most likely will travel overseas to serve in full-time medical missions. As the Mennonite pastor concluded in his sermon, "Giving her only son to God must not have been an easy thing for Hannah to do." I can only hope to draw strength from her example when the time comes for Clark to leave.

One way we can serve God is to remember that everything, including our children, is on loan from him. The Amish know that the Lord deserves our firstfruits, whether that consists of time, money, talents, or service. They are constantly examining their own lives for anything they are worshiping instead of God. We should do the same. We must continually pray to be released from the temptations of false idols, and instead—like Hannah—sing a song of joyful praise.

Serving the church

I have never witnessed a greater example of service to church than that displayed by our friend Mark. When we first started attending church, Mark invited us to faith group, which met each Wednesday evening at his home. Faith group was a collection of miscellany like us. We were new Christians, which is a dangerously zealous time. Christians should have their acts together, right? But these people were openly sharing their brokenness. Each week brought stories of wrecked marriages, lost jobs, tragic illnesses, and unwed motherhood. And we thought *our* lives were messed up!

When Matthew told Mark we were not getting much out of faith group, he immediately responded, "You are not here to get. You are here to give."

Through example, Mark taught us how to give. A single mom needed to get her kids away from a bad crowd, so she wanted to sell her trailer. Mark not only organized a crew to get the trailer spruced up to put on the market but found a safe and affordable place for her to live where she could be mentored by an experienced mom. A house cleaner had her beloved canoe stolen; Mark took up a collection, and the canoe was replaced within a week. A wife with three young children was dissatisfied with life and threw Dad out; Mark had the father move in with them for a couple of months and counseled him on reconciliation. A middle schooler seemed bent toward destruction; Mark took him under his wing, and now the boy is graduating with honors and hopes to become a physician.

Five years ago, our family moved out of state, but we keep in touch with our faith group and especially with Mark. When we got word that a member of the church had been in a fatal tractor accident leaving a wife and young family, the church not only brought in the crops but quickly took up a collection and provided a plan for long-term financial stability. As soon as we heard the news, Matthew called Mark to ask how we could help. Mark thanked us but said the church had already responded with so much generosity that the family's needs were met. I suspect he had a lot to do with that.

Widows and orphans. Unwed mothers. Reformed alcoholics, drug dealers, and criminals from the prison located just up the road from the church. These are just a few examples of needs the church was involved with. Though we were only members for a few years, our church taught us the important principle of service to others.

The Amish excel at serving their faith community. They give joyfully. Taking care of their church family is taken for granted—as normal as breathing. Service to church members is a source of gratification, not grief—a blessing rather than a burden.

Perhaps this, in part, is what Jesus meant when he said, "My yoke is easy and my burden is light" (Matthew 11:30, NIV). Salvation—the yoke—is easy. It is freely given. All you have to do is ask for it.

The burden—living the Christian life of service—is often the opposite of what we expect. It makes life lighter. It lessens the load. As we lift up our brothers and sisters in Christ, we are set free from the ills of isolation and loneliness.

Let's Sum It Up

The Amish understand that the key to a joyful life is simple: serve God; serve your neighbor. Interdependence can be more holy than independence. But how does that play out?

The Amish serve their children by doing the hard work of parenting, teaching them the skills and habits that will make them healthy spouses, colleagues, and neighbors. Instead of short-term distraction or coddling, they aim for long-term character and strength.

Through example, they show how caring for grandparents is a joy, not a burden. Likewise, service to neighbors and coworkers is treated more as an opportunity than an obligation. And service to one's own faith community is a chance to follow the example of Jesus, one act of compassion at a time.

In acting kind, we become kind. In serving others, we are served. Blessed are the merciful and the pure of heart. As the physical arms of God Almighty, we comfort those who mourn. In doing so, we serve him gladly, all the days of our lives.

CHAPTER 7

SECURITY

The only true security comes from God.

OUR DEAR FRIENDS Josh and Laura have been married only
a few years, and yet I don't know any couple more dedicated
to God, to their marriage, and to serving others. They are
full of joy, and one of the reasons is that they appreciate how
precarious life can be—Josh because of the untimely death
of his first wife, and Laura because of the trauma she wit-
nesses at work. Like my husband, Laura is trained as an ER
physician. One day recently they stopped by on their way to
a motorcycle dealer.

"Josh, you can't be serious," I blurted out. "A motorcycle?!
Your wife is an ER doctor!"

Josh deadpanned, "And I come from two generations of
funeral directors."

What a comeback! "But really, Josh, Matthew says they call them 'donorcycles' in the hospital. Laura needs you. We all need you."

Matthew came to my aid and added, "Be ye therefore wise as serpents, and harmless as doves" (Matthew 10:16, KJV).

"Amen!" Laura and I said in unison. Laura has a contagious laugh, and we all joined in. But the truth of these words from Jesus lingered in the room. Was I worrying unduly? Is it wrong to ride a motorcycle? Well, that's for us to decide for ourselves, but here's the real point: true faith in God does not put him to the test. Place your trust in God, yes! But don't take unnecessary risks.

Planning for the Unexpected

I come by my aversion to motorcycles honestly. Years ago, I was an office mate to a mother of three who rode motorcycles with her coal miner husband. Especially after his long shifts enclosed in dark and dank shafts, I'm sure their excursions felt like a foretaste of heaven.

A friend of mine here in Kentucky also rides motorcycles. An ordained minister in her early sixties who works at a seminary, she rides in back of her six-foot-five husband—with full leather protection and SPF 30 suntan lotion, of course—the ultimate fun, fit, and feisty grandma.

I am sure the majority of motorcyclists are, like these women and their husbands, prudent drivers. Yet when Josh mentioned getting a motorcycle, my mind immediately flashed back to the worst accident Matthew saw in all his years in the ER. Because of his training and experience with trauma, Matthew is accustomed to awful situations—or at least as accustomed as his compassion can allow. A young man falling off a three-story roof and becoming paralyzed, a child drowning in a public pool, a lobsterman carrying in his severed fingers—Matthew has seen it all.

But the worst by far was the time an animal ran out into the road among a large group of motorcyclists. One moment they were enjoying a fine morning in Maine, the next they were splattered all over the pavement. It was an ER physician's nightmare and a life-changing tragedy for dozens of spouses, parents, and children. The worst part: it could have been prevented. A little more space between motorcycles and a little less speed would have allowed the first cyclist to veer safely, without causing a pileup. The animal survived, but many of the cyclists did not. Once the chain reaction started, it could not be stopped.

As much as this event colored my view of them, motorcycles aren't really the issue here. The point is that bad choices tend to pile up on bad choices. Perhaps a seemingly random act—such as a dog running into the road or a corporate layoff or a government program cut—was the immediate cause of distress, but there are usually many independent decisions along the way over which no one has any control. The Amish approach: yes, walk in faith in God but also use the wisdom that he gave us to make good choices. So many of the disasters in our lives could be avoided if only we would heed the advice of Jesus to the apostles: retain the gentle innocence of a dove, but temper it with the cunning wisdom of the snake.

Security, Amish Style

The Amish, of course, do not drive motorized vehicles, two wheeled or otherwise. Living within horse-and-buggy distance is a limitation, but also a blessing. The payoff is a close-knit community where neighbors provide the security necessary to live a full and abundant life. By staying in a stable, secure community, they have been able to preserve a way of life that values a sense of place, both geographic and spiritual.

The Amish believe that security comes from God, not government or corporations. Those who expect the government or other institutions to take care of them risk bowing down to false idols. Scripture warns us not to follow the example of those who trust in man-made gods: "They worshiped worthless idols, so they became worthless themselves. They followed the example of the nations around them, disobeying the Lord's command not to imitate them" (2 Kings 17:15). Friends and family, acting as the hands and feet of God, are the best form of security.

Amish parents do not teach entitlement to their children, nor do they practice it themselves. Security comes from self-sufficiency, hard work, and careful stewardship of God's gifts. Faith in God, not faith in institutions or corporations, is the basis of all interactions.

Because they value stability, the Amish move far less

frequently than does modern society. Families tend to stick together. Neighboring families have known one another for generations. When moves do happen—such as when a compatible mate has not been found within the community or a young couple seeks farmland and it has become too scarce in their local area—they relocate to an Amish community that shares similar practices and values. More than likely, they will already have extended family or friends living in the new location to help welcome them. The "welcome buggy" includes many hands to help them move furniture in and introduce them to the new church family.

Even more important to the Amish than geographic stability is social stability. In their communities, things are done much like they were two and three generations back. Naturally some adjustments are made, but change happens at a much slower pace than the rest of us are accustomed to. This measured, deliberate approach to change, along with daily acknowledgment that true security comes only from God, leads to less angst and a deeper sense of stability.

Traditions of the major life ceremonies—birth, marriage, and death—remain nearly identical to those of their Swiss ancestors, and the ceremonial calendar is unchanging. For example, the *Attnungsgemee* (preparatory service) held two weeks before the semiannual Communion is a cleansing ritual where faults are confessed and differences between members are settled. In a similar way, Communion and foot washing follow the same patterns, generation after generation. Even the hymns chanted from the *Ausbund* have remained unchanged since the sixteenth century. Because the hymns appear without musical notations, all melodies are learned by ear and passed along from parents to children.

Tradition, stability, and sense of place are missing from most of our lives. The Amish recognize their importance, and foster the connection and security they provide. While true security ultimately comes from God, we can each make choices that prepare us for the difficult times all of us eventually must face.

Stormy Weather

When Matthew and I were courting, one of the first presents he gave me was a record album (how quaint!) by Willie Nelson. I still have it, and we still listen to it on the same thirty-plus-year-old record player. My favorite song on the album is "Stormy Weather." You are probably familiar with the lyrics, which have been recorded by Billie Holiday, Ella Fitzgerald, and many other greats. It begins,

> *Don't know why, there's no sun up in the sky.*
> *Stormy weather . . .*

The stormy weather in the song is a metaphor for a broken relationship between a man and a woman, but it could just as readily be about a broken relationship between man and God. The Amish, an agricultural society, know that all of us will go through stormy times in life—loss of friends, family, jobs, and health. The greatest storms come, however, not when a romance breaks up or a crop fails but when we lose touch with our greatest love, the Creator, who ultimately sustains and protects us all.

All I do is pray, the Lord above will let me
walk in the sun once more.

In good times and bad, we should turn first to "the Lord above." Here, the lyricist is in agreement with the Amish proverb: "God's hand that holds the ocean's depth can hold my small affairs. His hand, which guides the universe, can carry all my cares." The Amish trust in a God big enough to shoulder our concerns; they know he is the only true source of security.

King David, the bestselling songwriter of all time, experienced much "stormy weather" and recorded his pain and grief in the Psalms. Over and over again, David reminds us that in times of trouble, we must lean into God:

- I will call on God, and the LORD will rescue me. (Psalm 55:16)
- You alone, O LORD, will keep me safe. (Psalm 4:8)
- I know the LORD is always with me. I will not be shaken, for he is right beside me. (Psalm 16:8)
- The LORD is my fortress, protecting me from danger, so why should I tremble? (Psalm 27:1)
- Commit everything you do to the LORD. Trust him, and he will help you. (Psalm 37:5)

Unlike other literature of its time, the Bible records its heroes at their worst—adulterers, murderers, and more. But it also records them at their best. David, at his best, is in constant communication with God. Before taking any action, he asks God what to do. He is willing to risk his own life and the lives of thousands of his soldiers, even when the odds are heavily against them, simply because God told him to. He has the faith of a child.

This open line of communication, this absolute trust in God's wisdom even when the facts argue against the advice received, is why David is called a "man after God's own heart." Yes, David experiences stormy weather, but he trusts God to see him through. "Trusting God," as the Amish proverb points out, often "turns problems into opportunities."

Three Boats, One God

In ancient times, shipwrecks were much like the car wrecks of today. Most journeys ended uneventfully, but accidents were always a possibility—an undesirable but accepted risk in getting from point A to point B. It should not be surprising, then, that three of the most important stories in the Bible center on boating accidents.

Most of us are familiar with the story of Jonah. He is told to go to a foreign land, where people are very different from him. Although he's a prophet, Jonah balks. He's willing to do just about anything for God, but this is too far outside his comfort zone.

So when Jonah takes the first ship headed in the opposite direction, God conjures up a storm; the crew, finally believing that Jonah is the cause of all the fuss, throws him overboard. A great fish swallows Jonah, then spits him up on dry land. This time, Jonah follows God's orders, and the impossible happens: the people of Nineveh listen to Jonah, repent, and reform.

The second story involves Paul, the apostle to the Gentiles. Paul is on his way to Rome. The ship runs into some problems along the way, and Paul warns they'd better hole up for the winter. The crew does not listen. If they have to interrupt their journey, they'd rather vacation in a spiffier harbor. A huge storm hits. Paul prays, and God assures Paul that no one will perish. The ship falls apart, but—as God had promised—everyone makes it safely to shore.

In the third story, Jesus is crossing a lake with his friends. He's been working hard, and the motion of the water lulls him to sleep. A storm rises. The disciples get scared. They wake up Jesus, and he tells them not to fear. Jesus calms the storm, and they cross safely to the other side.

What do these three storm stories tell us? The story of Jonah reminds us that when confronted with a task far outside our comfort zones, our first reaction is to bolt. God, however, will always nudge us back, even if he has to send a whale-sized reminder.

The story of Paul reminds us that we often think we know better than God. When we try to follow our way rather than Yahweh's, bad things happen. God is the ultimate safety net.

The story of Jesus crossing the lake is a reminder that God is always beside us. If God can calm nature by simply saying "Be still," he can surely calm the fear and anxiety within our hearts.

The take-home message of all three shipwrecks: God is the only truly safe harbor.

The Almost Amish Way: Turn to God First for Security

How can the scripturally based, Amish attitude toward security be applied to our twenty-first-century lives? It's an ongoing journey, taken one step at a time. Here are a few ideas that may be of help along the way:

Get to know your neighbors

When we first moved to Kentucky, Matthew was traveling quite a bit. I immediately started teaching at a college two blocks from home and had met most of our neighbors, but Matthew barely unpacked and washed his clothes before he was back on the road again. He began to feel like a friendless nomad.

So I took some initiative. I invited colleagues and their spouses over for dinner. We began hosting weekly potlucks in the neighborhood. I kept animal crackers in the cupboard for the two-year-old next door, and she and her parents came over to give Matthew encouragement and hugs when he was home. Matthew was asked to guest teach a class at the local seminary, and one of the doctoral students took Matthew under his wing. Before we knew it, we had some of the deepest Christian friendships we had ever experienced.

These interactions with new neighbors quickly reminded me that it is as important to receive as to give. The first day we moved in, I asked my next-door neighbors if they had a ladder we could borrow. They invited us to dinner. We gladly accepted. Another neighbor offered us a step stool, and a third brought over lawn chairs so we would have someplace to sit in the evenings until our furniture arrived.

In later months, we were able to reciprocate with offers of child care, the lending of tools, and garden produce. When the neighbor who lent us a ladder had gall bladder problems in the middle of the night, she did not hesitate to call me to stay with their daughter. And when she continued to experience health problems throughout her second pregnancy, I was glad that they felt comfortable enough to leave their child in our care.

The Amish tend to live in the same community, generation after generation. There is great security in knowing not only the parents of your children's friends but their grandparents, uncles, and aunts. All of us go through hard times, and it is comforting to know that neighbors will be there to help.

In contrast, Americans move an average of 11.7 times in their lifetimes. Moves are difficult; they require finding new employment, new schools, new homes, and new plumbers. Most important, they require finding new church families and support networks.

Some moves are unavoidable, of course. If you have a

choice, consider staying put. And if you must move, invest immediately in the community. Even if you end up moving again, your relationships with God and neighbors will be richer.

Create an attractive family life

An attractive family life is one that makes other people, including your kids, want to hang out in your home. Your home becomes a haven to others and a slice of heaven for you.

Both Emma and Clark live in the same neighborhood we do and come over several times a week. They like hanging out with us. So do their friends. This does not happen by accident.

Part of the attraction is physical. Our town house is not large, but it is clean, uncluttered, and comfortable. People often tell us that they feel more relaxed the moment they step inside—so relaxed that many visitors have napped on our living room couches. Our home is a calming space.

Mostly, though, the attraction is relational. Matthew in particular was very conscious about raising our children to be people we'd want to spend time with as adults, and vice versa. We will always be their parents, but now we are also their companions.

One tradition that all of us make a priority is our Friday night family dinners. The kids invite friends, and together we celebrate the end of the week. Everyone is in the mood to kick back and relax. We've played board games, watched movies, gone bowling (in my case, two-handed gutter balls)—but mostly we eat, laugh, and talk. About half the time, we are celebrating someone's special occasion—a birthday, anniversary, or completion of a difficult semester. Always, we give thanks to God for the blessing of having family and friends who share both our struggles and our joys.

For the Amish, family meals and celebrations are the norm. Close proximity allows for easy and frequent interactions, and these in turn add richness to life. Having good times to balance out the bad contributes to a sense that family and friends will always be there for you, and you for them.

Weave tradition back into your life

The Amish are the Tevyes of tradition, à la *Fiddler on the Roof.* If it worked for their great grandfathers, they're in no rush to change. A simple example: the Amish traditional dress eliminates the need to keep up with changing fashions. Imagine how much less angst there would be if teens didn't have to worry about their tennis shoes being two minutes out of style! Yes, the Amish give up face piercings and tattoos, but these look dated and unattractive a decade later, anyway. Matthew says that nearly all his patients beyond the age of forty regretted their tattoos, but often could not afford the laser surgery to have them removed. Placing your security in God, not in the whims of collective cool, never goes out of fashion.

Below are ways you can deal tradition back into your life:

Food—Make ice cream "Sundays" your special Sunday

night dessert or cook initial pancakes (pancakes formed in the shape of the eater's initials) for Dad's Saturday morning breakfast. When I was growing up, on Friday night my mother served challah, a Jewish braided egg bread, lit candles to welcome the Sabbath bride, and said the blessing over the grape juice (which, believe me, is far tastier than kosher wine). But it doesn't have to be that elaborate either. Matthew grew up with home-raised chicken on Sundays. Many families have a regular pizza and movie night. Make your own edible traditions—comfort food in the truest sense.

Family night—In another interesting example of the "last shall be first" principle, surveys published by Child Trends Data Bank consistently show that the higher the income and education level, the less likely it is that a family will sit down to a meal together. Overall, a third of American families eat three or fewer meals together per week. In redefining what it means to be rich, perhaps the Amish example of sharing meals should be at the top of the list. At the very least, aim for one evening where everyone sits down together, and no one eats and runs. Although there may be resistance at first, the assurance that you will all reconvene one evening a week adds to everyone's sense of belonging and security.

Routine—Not all traditions have to center on food! Having a regular time to wake up, do chores, pray, work, and go to bed also builds in security. We know that children need consistency in order to feel safe and grow into healthy adults. Adults need routine too. If every day is a free-for-all, just-trying-to-get-by, survival-mode existence, then the bottom is always threatening to drop out. The Amish understand that, as children of God, we need routine to make breaking from the ordinary extraordinary. For instance, although barn raising involves long hours of hard work, it is different from the usual chores. Having a routine to break from makes such events particularly special.

Prayer—Not every family needs to pray in the same way, but every family needs to pray in some way. Pray alone, pray with your children, pray with a friend, pray with your spouse. Pray at work, pray at home, pray in the car, pray while you wait for the computer to reboot. The Bible tells us to pray ceaselessly. In the worst of times, we do; in the best of times, we often forget. The Amish recognize that the habit of prayer builds gratitude, humility, and security into our lives so that when the bad stuff happens, we know Whom to call first.

Don't expect institutions to solve all your problems

In the late seventies, I went to school in Lancaster County, Pennsylvania, the heart of Amish country. Matthew and I were dating long distance. He lived two hours away, near my parents.

On the radio one day, I started hearing reports about possible leakage from a nearby nuclear power plant. I called Matthew and told him that no one seemed in the least bit concerned. Students were sunbathing, joking about soaking in the radiation, and the officials on the news shows claimed that the public was in no danger. Nonetheless, I felt uneasy. So did Matthew. Because I didn't have a car, Matthew drove the two hours and brought me back home to my parents' house.

For the first few days, I felt guilty about missing school. By the end of the week, however, the college canceled classes, the government evacuated young children and pregnant women, and the utilities admitted to dumping radioactive material into the waterways.

The Amish do not rely on government or institutions to tell them what to do. They consult their elders, as the Bible tells us to do. Though Matthew is only four years my senior, he had considerably more real-world experience. When my parents concurred, I followed their collective advice. Without their input, I probably would have stayed on campus until the government or school officials evacuated us. After all, school was my job. I never missed classes.

The Amish accept almost no government assistance. We don't have to go that far, but—on the other extreme—neither should we wait for institutions to solve all our problems. Use common sense. Tap into your God-given wisdom. Exercise the free will that God gave to each of us. When you get anxious, turn to the ultimate Protector. He will lead you to still waters and help you take right action.

When life gets messy, turn to God FIRST

This should be the easiest principle to put into action, but for many of us, it's the hardest. No matter what you call the cause of our separation from God—"the Fall," or "evil," or

"Satan"—it's real and it's deadly. When stuff goes wrong, our knee-jerk reaction is to blame anyone but ourselves. We don't want to take responsibility, and we want someone else to bail us out.

The Amish understand that God is the answer to all life's problems. To help us, he left an instruction manual—the Bible. Abraham, Isaac, Jacob, the prophets, the apostles—they all turned to God when life got difficult. Even Jesus, in the Garden of Gethsemane, called out to God in his time of anguish.

The Amish, more than almost any other Christian denomination, consciously model their daily lives on the example of Jesus. They were practicing the "what would Jesus do" way of life centuries before it became popular. When Jesus was down, he turned to his Father—not self-help books, not web-med, not digital drugs. Nothing we can smoke, drink, or watch on TV will make our tribulations disappear permanently. No matter what the problem, God is the answer. Amish peace comes when we know this Truth not only in our minds but have inscribed it on the fleshy tablets of our hearts.

Let's Sum It Up

Half a century ago, Martin Luther King Jr. gave a sermon entitled "Paul's Letter to American Christians." In it, King warns that moral advances are not keeping abreast with our technological advances: "Through your scientific genius you have made of the world a neighborhood, but through your moral and spiritual genius you have failed to make of it a brotherhood."

We are all brothers and sisters in Christ. As the family of God, we must reach out to protect and care for others, even when it is inconvenient or costly. The most obvious opportunities for extending friendship, hospitality, and security are to those who live close by, and yet many of us spend far more hours in the portals of our virtual neighborhoods than on the porches of our neighbors. Less time in front of the computer screen means more time to spend on the town green.

The Amish build stability, routine, and tradition into their lives, all centered on God. We, too, can build a firm foundation based on an all-powerful, all-knowing, and all-loving God. Family and friends, acting as the hands and feet of God, can provide comfort along the way. Yet it is God—first, last, and always—who is the Truth, the Light, and the Way.

What does this look like in twenty-first-century terms? We can start by embracing the following:

- Encouraging routine. Too many decisions (at any age) can undermine security and become overwhelming. As countercultural as it may sound, boring is sometimes better.
- Staying put. If you have a choice, don't move. The security that comes from knowing neighbors, geography, and place can be worth far more than a pay raise.

- Taking responsibility. Sometimes when we're tempted to think of ourselves as victims, we actually need to blame less—and thank more.
- Setting boundaries. Margins of safety will increase your family's confidence and sense of belonging.
- Modeling stability. In marriage, parenting, and friendship, be the person that others can count on. The faster the world changes, the more the world needs you to be still and know/show that God is God.

Seeking security from money, power, and institutions may help in the short term, but ultimately we will end up disappointed. Amish peace is built upon the sure knowledge that the only true and lasting security comes from God.

CHAPTER 8

COMMUNITY

Knowing neighbors and supporting local businesses build community.

I'VE OFTEN HEARD IT SAID, "When the end of the world comes, head for Kentucky because it's always twenty years behind the times." Although this quip is not intended as a compliment, I have found that being behind the times can indeed have its advantages.

For five years, we lived in Wilmore, Kentucky, home of Asbury University and Asbury Seminary. Living two blocks from the center of town, I could walk everywhere—to work, the post office, the gym, the hair cutter, and the bank. Mr. Sims, the pharmacist, was the original owner of our house; Sims Drugs still bears his name and looks exactly as it did in the fifties, I'm told—complete with wooden dispensary and a lunch counter that serves heart-stopping milk shakes. Mai—owner of a downtown restaurant—piled our takeout into Tupperware that I brought over because she knows I prefer not to use throwaway containers. And then there is Fitch's IGA, the family-owned grocery store.

Mr. Fitch and his family have run the town grocery for fifty-five years. Like Sims Drugs, it has not changed much in those five decades. On multiple occasions, Matthew and I have witnessed the owner giving food to people in the checkout line who could not afford to pay, something that just does not happen in the typical chain grocery store.

Unfortunately, competition from supercenters up the road took its toll. Fitch's lost money for ten years. The store was teetering on closure when a group of neighbors got involved. Last Fourth of July, they picked up their pens to sign a "Declaration of Independence from Big Box Stores." Fitch's Neighbors, a grassroots volunteer group, pledged to purchase at least three meals a week from their local grocer.

That's not all. An Asbury Seminary student—inspired by his faith—organized an extreme grocery store makeover. Neighbors rolled up their sleeves on various projects, from scrubbing every inch of the store to completely repainting the exterior and a hundred small refurbishing touches in between. Together they logged more than six hundred people-hours to revitalize Fitch's. For the first time in a decade, the store is profitable again. Mr. Fitch says he never saw anything like it.

Neither have most of us, largely because family-owned stores are no longer the norm. Yet the example of Fitch's

Neighbors gives me great hope, a reminder that we don't have to be born into an Amish community to enjoy an Almost Amish life.

Local Is Better

Local economies thrive in Amish communities because the Amish support small, family-owned businesses. Although they are known for their frugality, friendship is valued more than lowest price. Because they do not drive, they depend on a robust local economy. It's in everyone's best interest for neighbors to support neighbors.

Unfortunately, such support and loyalty are dwindling in much of America. Soon after a supercenter moves in, the small-town grocery, hardware store, and pharmacy close. Consumers opt for so-called "bargains," which end up costing more than they could imagine: the life and livelihood of their town. The town begins to erode from the inside out.

Downtown gives way to box stores, and box stores mean many of us practically live in the car. No wonder we have become an exhausted nation, driving the equivalent of five cross-country trips per year and getting nowhere. In many communities, neighbors no longer borrow a cup of flour because no one stays home. Even if someone were at home, who has time to bake bread? And how can we "break bread together" and share a meal if all our friends are busy on Facebook?

I remember the first time a neighbor apologized for

knocking at our door. She said that she was sorry she had not called before coming by. This neighbor lived just a few houses away. Her kids were the same ages as mine. We carpooled together. Why, then, should she feel bad about stopping by in person?

At the other extreme, Matthew and I have lived in a house where neighbors regularly walked in without knocking. This was somewhat unnerving, especially since the bathroom was located right by the door. We never knew who we would meet when coming out of the shower.

Reaching a balance between too little and too much neighborly interaction can be tricky. On a societal level, however, the trend clearly seems to be in one direction: away from direct human contact. Stopping by has given way to telephone calls, which have been usurped by e-mail, which is being replaced by texting and tweeting, and there are new layers of protocol. Don't call unless you have a prearranged time to talk. Texting is noncommittal, but e-mail implies a nascent relationship. And heaven forbid that a long-lost friend should spontaneously stop by without making arrangements in advance. Of course, it's not the technologies that are inherently bad but how we choose to use them. In order to maintain healthy relationships, we must continually evaluate the role of new technologies in our lives. If we increasingly use technology to separate us from human contact, red flags should go up.

As I said earlier, the Amish joke that their favorite sport is visiting. And instead of parallel play (pursuing separate activities together), they engage in conversation. Without telephones or computers, visits cannot be pre-arranged by phone, e-mail, or texting. Stopping by is not considered an intrusion; it is a welcome respite in a work-filled week. Instead of conducting business on the doorstep, the Amish invite visitors in—physically and spiritually. According to an Amish proverb, face-to-face contact with a friend is "like the rainbow that is always there for you after the storm." In our alienated and often lonely world, we could learn much from the Amish example of community.

Living in Community

Two German terms, *Gelassenheit* and *Ordnung*, are at the center of Amish community life. Gelassenheit, often translated as "self-surrender to a higher authority," is basically submission. And it's important to note that submission is based on respect. Children obey their parents, students their teachers, church members their leaders, and younger ministers their bishop. The highest authority is God. This strong emphasis on Gelassenheit results in a great respect for the dignity of each person.

Submission, self-surrender, and yielding to the will of others is the inverse of modern American culture. We live in an excessively individualistic society. Originality is king; we worship trendsetters. Frank Sinatra crooned our theme song: We insist on doing it *our* way.

Yet the Amish understand that self-concern at any cost is,

well, costly. Instead of feeling content with what we have, we must always strive for the latest and greatest. We rank individualism above the welfare of the community. The result: we have an anxious, easily distracted, and unsettled nation where the opinion of one person—espoused through Twitter, talk radio, or blogs—is valued more than the collective wisdom of the community. While some believe that blogs build community, the Amish would likely say that such community is shallow—a shadow of the real thing. As Wheaton College professor and former blogger Alan Jacobs aptly put it, blogging is the "friend of information but the enemy of thought." The Amish value millennia-old, biblical precepts more than progress at any price.

The second central tenet of community life is Ordnung, which means "order." The Ordnung encompasses community-specific regulations passed on through practice and tradition. These regulations, usually unwritten, apply the biblical call for separation from the world to community life—from grooming, clothing, and recreation to transportation, technology, and education. For example, in Amish communities dress is a symbol of group identity, not a means of personal expression.

In that regard, the Ordnung shares some similarities with rabbinic law: Hassidic communities apply specific laws in different ways, yet to non-Jews their black-rimmed hats, long side curls, and somber, dark coats make them appear all the same. Likewise, although the Amish appear similar to outsiders, the Ordnung varies among their more than two dozen affiliates. These affiliates fall into four major categories:

Beachy Amish, Amish Mennonites, New Order Amish, and Old Order Amish. As an example, the Ordnung for Beachy Amish and Amish Mennonites allows automobile ownership and public utility electricity, while the Old Order and New Order Amish prohibit both.

During the adult baptism ceremony, members agree not only to follow Christ but also to obey the community's Ordnung. If they subsequently break that vow, they can be subject to church discipline. While many outsiders see shunning as the darkest side of Amish life, in practice it is balanced by opportunities for forgiveness and grace. The decision to observe the rules of the community is made as an adult, with eyes wide open. If a member later reneges, there are clear consequences—akin to "tough love." In most districts, the Amish follow the process recommended by Jesus (Matthew 18:15-17) of approaching the offender in private, then with a group of elders; in addition, some communities allow another six months to a year for the person to confess and change before instituting discipline. Even after excommunication, the person can repent and all will be forgiven. In the non-Amish world, such unconditional grace is more than many of us extend, even to our spouses and families!

Gelassenheit and Ordnung sound restrictive. And they are, which is exactly why the Amish value them. It would be easy to misinterpret this desire as some draconian impulse, but the Amish simply believe that setting and respecting limits is essential for both community and individual happiness. As modern American society has shown, "anything goes" often leads to reckless, self-destructive behavior.

The Amish believe that limiting choice enhances dignity and security. A respect for limits builds community, creates a sense of belonging, and shapes identity—three important keys that are largely missing in our modern world.

The Almost Amish Way: Knowing Your Neighbor and Supporting Local

The Amish build community the same ways we do, only more so: by supporting the local economy, being involved in community schools, participating in the district church, welcoming neighbors into their homes, and enjoying local, noncommercial recreation. By intentionally building community, they greatly reduce many social problems—such as isolation, homelessness, and unemployment. Below are some ways we can adopt Almost Amish attitudes and practices that build strong communities.

Shop local, local, local

For a couple of years, I lived in Lancaster County, the heart of Amish country. One of the things that struck me was the number of businesses with family names. Kauffman's, Miller's, Snyder's, Gish's, Yoder's, Zook's—these are family businesses, supporting and supported by their neighbors.

Though it may take a little more effort, you don't have to live in an Amish community to find local businesses. When you eat out, for example, do you play it safe at a franchise or do you check out independent restaurants, unique to your community? When you go to the barber or hairdresser, do you seek out an independent operator? Does your bank have just a few local branches, or is it part of a national conglomerate? Bakeries, hardware stores, shoe stores, movie theaters, produce stands, plumbers, electricians, laundries, general contractors, dentists, optometrists, ice cream shops, booksellers, gift shops, stationers, clothing stores—these are just a few of the local businesses in my neighborhood that I can choose to support, or not support, every time I need goods or services. Instead of whining about a dying downtown, I can put my wallet to work.

Do I like the convenience of buying everything in one store? Of course, and I like the generally lower prices too. But at what cost? Local jobs, a healthy downtown, knowing the grocery clerk by name? Our banker actually started keeping lollipops at the front desk, just for my husband. Such relationships are priceless. If it takes me a few extra minutes or a few extra dollars to promote the health of my community, I should be willing to make the investment.

While you may not be able to fathom Mayberry, the idyllic small town of 1960s TV, at one time or another you probably experienced exceptional personal service in a small shop—the barista who remembers how you take your coffee, the dry cleaner who knows you like your shirts folded and not hung, the hairdresser who remembers to ask about your ailing parent. When we experience extraordinary service, we should tell our friends and reward it with our loyal patronage.

Of course, as a follower of Christ, I have another reason to value community over convenience: because it is a biblical principle. Think of Ruth, the Moabite widow. In staying beside her mother-in-law, Naomi, she was joining a community—"Your people will be my people, and your God will be my God" (Ruth 1:16). This choice involved travel. It involved financial hardship. It involved hard work in the fields. But in return, the community—as characterized by the generosity of Boaz—took care of these two penniless widows.

The same principles are demonstrated in the book of Acts: "All the believers were united in heart and mind. And they felt that what they owned was not their own, so they shared everything they had" (Acts 4:32). When people in the early church saw a need, they met it. Luke, the author of Acts, makes it clear that people shared all things in common, not because it was easy or self-serving, but because it was the loving thing to do. In other words, they supported one another financially, not because it was convenient, but because it was best for the community as a whole.

Anyone who has lived in an organized community—for instance, a dorm, an apartment, or a homeowner's association—knows that personal convenience must sometimes be sacrificed for the good of the community. You might enjoy listening to music with the volume turned up, but your neighbor below does not. You may want to have a pet but decide against it because the people next door would not appreciate the dog barking while you are at work all day. But sacrifice, too, is biblical—as we can see in Matthew 22:37-40 (loving God by loving neighbors), Romans 12:3-13 (the body of Christ acting together in love), and Galatians 6:2 (obeying the law of Christ by sharing each other's burdens).

Similar principles apply to supporting a local economy. It might be more convenient for you to get your groceries, eyeglasses, manicure, and gas grill all in the same store, but there are costs that do not scan into the cash register or print out on your receipts. Those costs might be your neighbors' livelihood, which eventually translate to empty storefronts and foreclosed homes. Instead, intentionally seek out businesses located within a couple miles of your house that are not part of a chain and stop in at least one each week to learn about what they do. Once you are familiar with some of these local stores and their owners, make an effort to do business with them and recommend them to others.

The Amish have a saying: "Community is like an old coat—you aren't aware of it until it is taken away." Despite their reputation for frugality, the Amish understand that the lowest unit price is not always the least costly choice. We can apply their example by purchasing our goods and services at local businesses, beginning now.

Get involved in community schools

I recently went back to visit the neighborhood where we raised our kids. As I walked around the block with a former neighbor, I asked for an update on the families. Although almost no one had moved away, my friend had lost touch with many of them. She attributed this lack of connection to their children's no longer attending school together. Once the kids were grown and out of school, the neighbors lost the thread that had connected them on a day-by-day basis.

For many of us, local schools are the nexus for our sense of community. The Amish are no exception. Before 1950, most Amish attended small, local public schools. But as rural schools began consolidating, the Amish chose to remain local. Today, the majority of Amish youth attend one- or two-room schools that are operated by Amish parents. A local board of three to five fathers organizes the school, hires a teacher, approves the curriculum, oversees the budget, and supervises maintenance. Every aspect of schooling the young is a community affair.

Perhaps the most well-known example of an Amish community being pulled together by a school incident took place in Lancaster County in 2006. A man who interacted with the Amish community as a milk collector, Charles Roberts, took hostages in the West Nickel Mines one-room schoolhouse and shot ten girls, ages six to thirteen. Five of these young Amish girls died. The gunman then committed suicide, leaving behind his own young family.

Matthew and I recently watched a movie based on this horrific act of violence. While some artistic aspects may not be Oscar quality, the story of community and forgiveness is so compelling that I would rate it as one of the most memorable movies I have ever seen. I later learned that I am not alone. With more than four million viewers, the premiere of *Amish Grace* became the highest-rated and most-watched original movie in Lifetime Movie Network's history.

The heart tug of this story can be summarized in one word: redemption. Out of an evil act, good has come. The Amish have become a living example of a community of forgiveness. Within hours of the shooting, Amish neighbors began reaching out to the gunman's widow and three children. They set up a fund to support the young family. They comforted both the gunman's parents and parents-in-law. Thirty people from this small Amish community even attended the gunman's funeral.

In an open letter of appreciation, the widow thanked the Amish community: "Your love for our family has helped to provide the healing we so desperately need. Gifts you've given have touched our hearts in a way no words can describe. Your compassion has reached beyond our family, beyond our community, and is changing our world, and for this we sincerely thank you."

Within a week of the shooting, the Amish schoolhouse was demolished. Exactly six months later, the community completed a new building and named it New Hope School.

That is what the Amish offer all of us: new hope for our children, our communities, and the Kingdom of God, where forgiveness, grace, and mercy shall reign. While our involvement in community schools will likely take a less dramatic form—volunteering in the classroom, mentoring a struggling student, offering after-school homework help—these are nonetheless powerful opportunities to strengthen our communities and share God's love.

Participate in your community church

The Amish view church as a body of people, not a building. Yet even more than the most beautiful cathedral, church is at the core of the Amish community.

Church services are held every two weeks in someone's home. The location rotates, but the ceremonies, songs, and traditions remain unchanged. Worship time is followed by a community meal.

Unlike the outside world, "church shopping" is unheard of. You attend the church in your district, period—usually for life. One reason is purely practical: without cars, church hopping becomes problematic. But the main reason is more philosophical: worship is about God, not us.

A friend recently told me about a discussion between his pastor and a member of the congregation. The member told the pastor that he really enjoyed the sermon, but the songs that week weren't so great. "The worship today just didn't do much for me."

The pastor's response: "I'm sorry to hear that, but the worship wasn't meant for you. It's for God." That may sound harsh, but it's a message many of us need to hear.

Not so long ago, church membership was like a marriage. For better and for worse, you stuck together. This commitment to the long haul contributed to the sense of community.

Like marriages and so many other parts of modern life, however, churches have become disposable. If they no longer fit our needs, we move on. Many people approach church like a blind date: Which church has the best child care? Which church plays my favorite style of music? Which church has the strongest recreation program? Which church has the prettiest sanctuary? I also often hear stories of "church dipping"—attending one church for spiritual food, one for doing community outreach, another for the children's Sunday school program. There's nothing wrong with looking for a good fit when we move to a new town, just as there is nothing wrong in searching for the right spouse while we are single. The problem comes when we become a church critic—unwilling to commit to a body of people who can hold us accountable, nurture us, and provide opportunities to serve the community of faith.

In a letter to the Corinthians, Paul speaks of using our spiritual gifts for "the common good" (1 Corinthians 12:7, NIV). The Amish understand that we need church both to build community and "to motivate one another to acts of love and good works" (Hebrews 10:24). Most of all, church, in its many forms, provides us with opportunities to "do good to everyone—especially to those in the family of faith" (Galatians 6:10).

These acts of love and good works are usually best done in a stable, local community of believers who understand the specific needs and the gifts of their neighbors. History gives context, and context decreases the likelihood of people falling through the cracks. Sticking with a local church, even when we are tempted to leave, requires commitment and loyalty, two necessary attributes for any body of believers to thrive.

If you are not already a member of a church, visit those that are closest to your home. Once you commit to a church, see if they have a small group you can join.

Welcome others into your home

Last weekend, we had three different groups of friends, new and old, break bread with us. The first were friends from New England, dropping their son off at college and staying with us overnight. The next was a longtime friend from Nashville, in town for a workshop. He slipped out during the midday break to have lunch with us. The third group consisted of family and friends of family, some of whom we had never met before. Hosting these visitors was a privilege, the benefit to our family far outweighing any inconvenience of "having" to feed those who stopped by.

Matthew and I view opening our home to others as a joyous responsibility and a central part of building community. My motivation, especially when I'm doing the dishes afterward, comes from the letter to the Hebrews: "Don't forget to show hospitality to strangers, for some who have done this have entertained angels without realizing it!" (Hebrews 13:2). I am also inspired by the example of the Amish.

The Amish are productive, hardworking people, but they enjoy visiting. Hospitality is built into the regular rhythm and rituals of their lives. Church, as I have mentioned, does not happen in a separate building—it rotates among the members' homes and always includes a meal for a hundred or so family and friends. Wedding receptions, likewise, occur not in a hotel or hired reception hall, but in the home. Adult baptism and the semiannual Communion, an eight-hour affair that includes foot washing and a shared meal, are ritual high points of the year—and (you guessed it!) all take place in someone's home. Visiting, quilting bees, and "frolics," where work and play are combined, all involve hospitality.

Recently, Matthew and I attended a neighborhood corn bread supper. The tradition was begun years ago by our neighbors. Each Monday evening, they bake several varieties of corn bread and open their home to the neighborhood. Everyone brings a dish, with an emphasis on local and in-season foods.

Newcomers learn the ropes pretty quickly: there's one table for main dishes, one for drinks, one for desserts. A stack of paper squares and pencils is left on the table for people to put a place card by their dish, identifying any local ingredients and giving helpful information—"contains nuts," "gluten-free," "spicy!" Several groupings of chairs are arranged throughout the first floor and on the ample porch. In the kitchen, there is a bowl for leaving your used cloth napkins, a bowl for food scraps (so they can be composted later), and a space to stack dishes. When the stack gets high enough, someone will rinse plates and start the first load running in the dishwasher.

I have met some incredibly generous neighbors at the corn bread suppers. One new friend, a retired human resources manager, offered to help with our growing nonprofit's employee manual—and ended up writing it for us. Another young friend lets me French braid her hair—she loves the braided challah I make, and I love having a little girl's waist-length brown locks to work with. I've met writers, urban farmers, pastors, university officials, and grad students—of every age and background. While the couple who host are not Amish, I certainly consider their weekly hospitality a beautiful example of the Almost Amish way of life.

Have fun, locally

What do the Amish do for fun? Or, as one friend asked me, do the Amish even know how to have fun? The Amish work hard, but they also enjoy breaks from the routine of work. Because they do not drive or consume most forms of digital distraction, recreation among the Amish focuses on local activities, often involving nature. Having farm chores that require them to stay close to home, Amish families are more tied to the local community. Swimming, camping, fishing, and hunting in summer and sledding, skating, and ice hockey in winter provide breaks from the work routine. Informal games such as volleyball, softball, and corner ball are favorites in many Amish communities. Camping in local forests and meadows is also popular in some districts.

Barn raisings, work bees, and monthly gatherings when sisters, mothers, and aunts can produce or do other seasonal chores together are important social events that weave together work and leisure. In a similar way, group sings blend worship and pleasure in most Amish communities. Such activities within church districts incorporate fun activities into the larger social and spiritual framework.

Almost without exception, Amish leisure does not involve recreational shopping, prepackaged entertainment, or other commercial pursuits. It connects people to one another and the outdoors. It is almost always community oriented, revolving around family and friends.

In our modern world, downtime tends to separate people rather than bring us together. We engage more with our computers, TVs, and earphones than we do with our neighbors. While the Amish spend significantly less money on high-tech toys, they experience a richer form of fun. Making an effort to attend local festivals, picnicking in the parks, and engaging in informal socializing are simple ways we can build community while having a good time.

Still need a few more ideas to get you going? You can

- Play together. If you have young children, find a few neighbors who might want to get together on a regular basis to share child care and have some adult time while the kids play.
- Turn your yard or an open space into a center of fun. Horseshoes, badminton, a tire or rope swing, and other old-fashioned games can be a magnet for pulling neighborhoods together.

- Begin a book group. One great way to expand your mind and get to know your neighbors is through a monthly reading group. If you can't find one, start one!
- Invite neighbors for a meal. Breaking bread together is one of the best ways to break down barriers. To maximize enjoyment, let go of any expectations of a return invitation, and don't be shy about allowing others to bring salad or dessert.
- Walk the talk. It could be just two or three friends that meet at a regular time to get some fresh air while catching up on each other's lives. I've found walks to be one of the best ways to have uninterrupted conversations with friends and neighbors.

Most of all, be friendly. Knock on your neighbor's door. Reach out. Don't wait for the other person to make the first move. As the Amish like to say, "The most beautiful attire is a smile."

Let's Sum It Up

The Amish have avoided many of our social ills because they build community into their lives. People know and care about one another. They support one another's businesses, worship together, take an active role in their children's education, welcome neighbors into their homes, and engage in group activities to break up the routine of work. Because of this emphasis on community, virtually no members are homeless, unemployed, or living on government subsidies. Almost no Amish people are incarcerated, and rarely do Amish couples divorce.

By submitting to a higher authority, they keep the focus on the Ultimate Authority. This submission to God makes getting seem less important and giving more rewarding. The happiness of the community contributes to the happiness of the individual, and vice versa.

Here's the good news: the power of community is not limited to those born Amish. It can start with you, in your neighborhood, beginning today.

CHAPTER 9

FAMILIES

Family ties are lifelong; they change but never cease.

A FEW YEARS into our simplicity journey, a physician approached Clark at church and asked about his college plans. When Clark mentioned an Ivy League school, the doctor asked, "Why would you want to go there?" He went on to tell Clark about his alma mater, explaining that Clark could still meet his goal of becoming a physician but would have a much richer spiritual life if he attended a Christian college.

On the way home from church, Clark—who rarely asks for anything—wanted to know if he could go see Asbury, the college the doctor had described. We made arrangements for Clark and Matthew to visit. They attended chapel, sat in on several outstanding classes, and met with students and professors. At the end of the weekend, sitting in the college parking lot, father and son prayed together. Both returned home knowing that Asbury was where Clark should be.

Like many calls from God, at first their choice did not seem to make worldly sense. I adjusted quickly to the Christian college idea, but did it have to be in Kentucky? We didn't know a soul there, and it was so far away—in the South! Besides, Clark already had scholarship offers from other schools. Our family had taken a big leap of faith when Matthew left his ER position. Was this another test from God?

Despite my initial concerns, Clark matriculated at Asbury. God worked out the financial details via an academic award, and it quickly became clear that Clark's prayers for spiritual growth and preparation for calling were being answered— beyond our boldest prayers.

During Clark's freshman year at Asbury, Emma visited and felt called to go to college with her brother. Now, Emma does not always follow the typical path. For example, she wrote a book on creation care and had it published by a major Christian publisher while she was still in her mid-teens; and, instead of doing her senior year of high school in the usual way, she hoped to volunteer at an orphanage in Guatemala. (We nixed that idea because of her age, but she held onto the dream and later spent a semester serving in India.) God has accomplished much through her young life. So, after a lot of prayer, we gave her the green light to look into applying to Asbury a few months after her college visit. The hitch: she was only fifteen. Asbury said they would consider her application, but she needed to take her SATs first. She aced them. They invited her to their scholarship weekend. Asbury offers one entering freshman boy and one girl a four-year full ride.

At the ripe old age of fifteen and a half, Emma not only was accepted to college but was awarded a free education. This seemed to be an answer to the how-to-pay-for-two-kids-in-college question, but Matthew said it was too early to break up the family. His solution: we would all relocate to Kentucky.

At first, I resisted. I had an ideal teaching job, good friends, and a supportive church community. But it did not take long for Matthew to convince me that—after God—family comes first.

We asked the kids how close to Asbury they wanted us to move. "Within walking distance of campus" was their answer. Parental hovering? Perhaps, but our children were both quite young when we made the decision—fifteen and seventeen—and still wanted us around. Besides, neither had their driver's license yet. During the school year, they lived in the dorms, but a hug and a home-cooked meal were never more than ten minutes away.

In God's perfect plan, moving to the Bible Belt turned out to be the best thing we ever did for both our ministry and our marriage. After the first year, we had so many new friends supporting us and so many speaking requests that I left teaching to help launch our nonprofit, Blessed Earth. As a family, we discerned a clear, shared calling that blended our complementary gifts, all for his glory.

After Emma's graduation, Matthew and I discussed the possibility of moving back to New England. By this time, yet another of Clark's prayers had been answered: for a God-centered relationship with a lifelong mate. We now had a new member of the family to consider, our daughter-in-law, Val.

Because our house was so close to campus, I had the privilege of getting to know Clark's college sweetheart for three years before they married. At Val's request, on Thursday afternoons we cooked together, preparing some of Clark's favorite recipes while swapping family stories. Val and Emma were in the same graduating class at Asbury and were already "sisters," having served together in India their junior year. Val's family lived just up the road in Lexington. Although our family had grown and changed, our commitment to each other was stronger than ever.

So instead of moving back to New England, we moved to a town house in Lexington. Now adults, our children still (miraculously) enjoy being around us. Clark, twenty-three, married, and in his last year of medical school, lives five blocks from us. Emma, twenty-one, lives with her college roommate five blocks in the other direction. We get together on Friday evenings for family dinners, and Clark, Val, and Emma all stop by throughout the week for walks and talks.

I can say without hesitation that Matthew and Clark have the closest and most respectful father-son relationship I have ever seen. A central part of that bond is their shared love of medicine. Clark often runs his patients by Matthew, and Matthew enjoys passing along the art of healing. While this could be done via e-mail or phone, it's exponentially more rewarding for both to share these conversations sitting together in Matthew's study.

As fellow English majors, Emma and I share a love for Scrabble and the underappreciated semicolon. Emma is a fabulous writer and editor and now uses her abundant gifts to support our creation-care ministry. It brings me tremendous joy to have her working beside me—her passion, intelligence, and creativity are irreplaceable. Truly, I cannot imagine how I ever got by without her, and our shared vocation now adds another layer of depth to an already extraordinary relationship. Just as an Amish farmer might pass along wisdom and knowledge to the next generation, Matthew and I each share a professional bond with our children.

Old-fashioned? You bet. There is much to be said for the Almost Amish blessing of proximity. What a gift not only to love your grown children but to truly like and admire them, and for them to like and admire you in return.

Amish Traditions

Unlike most modern Americans, the vast majority of Amish families have remained intact. By staying geographically close and continuing to observe centuries-old traditions, they have avoided many of the ills of modern society. Within Amish communities, the divorce rate is less than one percent, illegitimate births are nearly unheard of, and the suicide rate is about half the American average. Families take care of their disabled and elderly relatives, and men and women have clearly defined roles. Even where farming is no longer the primary source of income, families often work together in a home-based business.

Because the Amish do not drive, everyone tends to keep close to home. This means families eat most meals together, children are not running off to after-school activities, and couples work in tandem. Amish independence from technology means that leisure time brings them closer, rather than driving them apart. Instead of being wired to digital entertainment, they spend downtime together.

Not being dependent on cars or technology also has significant health benefits. Walking and physical activity are built into Amish lives. Tending horses, gardens, and woodpiles keeps family members together while keeping them healthy. According to a study at the University of Tennessee, only 4 percent of the Old Order Amish suffer from obesity, compared to 33 percent—a third—of the American mainstream population.

Health and well-being are central to all aspects of Amish family life. When parents have differences, they discuss them in private. Couples do not air their disagreements in front of others. Children are expected to speak and act with respect toward elders, and adults model respectful behavior in and out of the home.

The Amish transition from dependence (childhood), to independence (adolescence), to interdependence (adulthood) includes a period called *rumspringa*. In many Amish communities, rumspringa is a time when adolescents are allowed greater freedom. During rumspringa, many youth experiment with worldly behaviors, such as driving a car, wearing modern clothes, watching TV, and going to the movies. Teens are not under the authority of the church until they choose to be baptized, sometime after the age of eighteen. Following this brief fling with worldly activities, most Amish young adults return to the church. Because the decision is theirs, the period of rumspringa ultimately strengthens their lifelong commitment to family and faith.

A common theme of these Amish traditions is harmony. Instead of family members working against one another, they work together. What is good for the family is considered good for the individual, and vice versa.

Learning from the Good Examples

When my husband was in residency, I read a local newspaper report on the rapidly rising caesarean section rates. Contrary to the trend, the C-section rate at my husband's hospital was one of the lowest in the state.

Here's what I found intriguing, and disturbing, about the article: the reporters only conducted interviews at the hospitals with the highest C-section rates and never looked for the solutions at the hospitals with the lowest rates. Think about that for a moment: they looked for answers where things were going wrong instead of where things were still going right.

The C-section rate was low at my husband's hospital, not because of high-tech medicine but because of two old-fashioned principles: first, doctors were still skilled in the

art of manually manipulating babies, so that breech pre-
sentations were rare. Second, the hospital had resisted the
trend toward nearly universal administration of epidurals,
which can slow or even halt labor. When I was pregnant with
Emma, I knew that the birthing process would be painful,
but I also knew that I was unlikely to end up in the operat-
ing room, which seemed like a pretty good trade-off to me.

In a similar way, perhaps we should begin to look for ways
to build healthy families where things are still going right.
According to the National Center for Health Statistics, more
than 40 percent of births in America are to unwed mothers.
Although it is commonly acknowledged that 50 percent of
marriages end in divorce, what these stats do not take into
account are the households where couples live together outside of marriage, blending and breaking up makeshift families
seemingly at will. Surrounded by adult role models saying one
thing and doing another, young people are losing faith in everything, including the church. Little wonder that, according to a
recent Barna study, more than 40 percent of our young people
leave the church between the ages of eighteen and thirty.

Instead of helplessly sitting by and watching the stats continue to slide in the wrong direction, wouldn't it make sense
to identify what *is* working and look for solutions there?

The Almost Amish Way: Family Ties Are Lifelong

What are some of the factors that keep the Amish family
together? Below are some Almost Amish actions you might

want to incorporate in your life—simple steps "backward" that can help us reverse some family-destroying trends.

Stay close geographically

The big promise of many ads for telephone and Internet services is that we can "stay connected." To some extent, this is true—Facebook, e-mail, texting, and smart phones can help us keep track of family and friends. Yet it is a Silicon Valley/Madison Avenue/Hollywood-propagated falsehood that digital communication can replace real-time, real-space interactions. A little emoticon can never duplicate a little child's hug.

Matthew, Emma, and I recently led a weekend of workshops at a small church in Nashville. The church is adjacent to Vanderbilt University, and the congregation probably has the highest ratio of degrees per pew than any other we have visited. Throughout our workshop discussions, we repeatedly heard people complain that technology has become their master. These young adults, mostly in their twenties or early thirties, were striving for community and earnestly seeking Christ-centered lives. With families dispersed, Facebook had become a poor substitute for real-time relationships. Some confessed that they had difficulty relating other than digitally. Couples who had met online spoke about how after dating long-distance they had a hard time adjusting to the reality of personal quirks and face-to-face interactions.

Children need freedom to make choices and grow into

independent adults, but do they need to be divorced for decades from the wisdom and loving support of family? Perhaps we can learn something from the Amish tradition of rumspringa, providing a way for young people to test the waters and then *choose* to come back—or rather, to stay. For many young people, attending a church-based summer camp, serving overseas between high school and college, participating in a program such as Mission Year, or matriculating in a Christian college provides room to stretch and grow within a nurturing environment.

Other young people seek wider latitude, including—unfortunately—the freedom to make some life-altering bad choices. To reach out to those who have rejected the church, one couple we know has recently started a ministry specifically for eighteen- to twenty-eight-year-olds. At the first meeting, they opened their home to more than forty young people. Many had made poor decisions during their "rumspringa," which led to relationships with abusive boyfriends, unwed motherhood, and unhealthy addictions. This couple embraces each of them with love, providing mature mentoring and a space for redemption. What a beautiful ministry! As James says in the last line of his epistle, "If someone among you wanders away from the truth and is brought back, you can be sure that whoever brings the sinner back will save that person from death and bring about the forgiveness of many sins" (James 5:19-20).

My husband and kids are artistically gifted, and art has always played a central role in our family's life. One of my all-time favorite paintings is Rembrandt's *The Return of the Prodigal Son*. The wayward child, returning to his family home, is on his knees with his head resting against his father's chest. The father is bent over with hands encircling him, at once gentle and almost motherly as well as strong and paternal. The father is not rebuking the son; he is not demanding explanations. The message that Rembrandt seems to be sending is that physical proximity is, for the moment, enough.

The scene reminds me of Emma when she was little. After her bath, I would wrap her in a white towel, and she would lean her head against me as I rubbed her wet mass of curly locks. Neither of us needed to say anything. The smell of her shampoo, the warmth of her cheek, the certainty that I could bear her weight as she leaned into me was all we needed to be content.

People speak of a "ministry of presence." What better place to practice this ministry of presence than in our own families? Like the Amish young adults after rumspringa, many of us can make choices to bring family together rather than allow jobs, schooling, and chance to separate us indefinitely. And when distance does separate us, we can make efforts to come together in real time and real space to renew our ties and create new memories.

Share family meals

Sharing meals is an act of intimacy. It creates bonds that are essential to preserving a healthy marriage and family life.

Many Amish families share three meals a day, a key factor in keeping their relationships healthy.

If I could start life over, there are many things that I would do differently, but making family meals a priority is one thing I would not change. From a very early age, the kids were taught to help with meal preparation, set the table, pour water, and do dishes. Making dinner was not drudgery but a way of coming together. I enjoyed taking the kids with me to the grocery store; they were a help in loading and unloading groceries and I never worried about them begging for treats or misbehaving. From the Amish example I have learned that if we maintain high expectations, our children will rise to them.

I recently met a college student who grew up with a single parent. Her mother had to work long hours, so eating dinner together was not an option. While this young woman admitted she "never ate at home," she always ate with family. Because her grandparents lived just down the street, she was welcome at their table. And her best friend came from a family with eleven children, so another place setting at the home of her "adopted family" was almost a daily occurrence. While being raised by only one parent is not ideal, it warmed my heart to know that this very Christ-centered, cheerful young woman always knew she had a place at the table.

Matthew and I are fortunate to be part of a group of couples who meet regularly to eat, pray, and talk about God. One of these dear couples is comprised of a physician and her artist husband, who works out of the studio behind their home. Family meals are a huge priority for both of them, but the demands of her medical practice began to take their toll. So, by mutual agreement, the husband began to cook, both as a creative outlet and as a family-building activity. At first, it was difficult for my friend to let go and allow her husband space in the kitchen. Her husband is now an accomplished chef, and—after cutting back on her medical practice—they have learned to enjoy cooking together. The result: more time together as a family and wholesome food for their bodies, minds, and spirits.

Respect gender roles

Just as each family situation is unique, the Amish community at large encompasses a spectrum of behaviors. We benefit most when we look at their example with an open mind and heart—especially when encountering some of their traditions that run most strongly against the mainstream today. Few would argue with the notion that Amish families are intact in part because they respect traditional gender roles.

Believe me, I know. When I speak at seminars, I am all too aware that the immense change in gender roles over the last half century is the elephant in the room that no one wants to talk about—at least, not in any depth. While some changes have been for the good, many have had unintended negative consequences. Irrespective of your personal views on feminism and the women's movement, we cannot ignore the large part that traditional gender roles play in keeping Amish families together.

For a year, I taught a combined kindergarten-through-third-grade class, the Almost Amish equivalent of a one-room schoolhouse. Teachers are not supposed to have favorites, but who could not love Alexander? He was a bundle of five-year-old affection, intelligence, and curiosity. When he entered the classroom each morning, I felt energized by his full-press hug.

Although he was loving and compassionate, Alexander had one fascination that puzzled me. Every time we went to the library, he picked out books about war. Every time he drew a picture, it was of a soldier or a weapon. Every time he dictated a story to me, it involved a battle. I often played classical music while the children worked quietly. One day, Alexander asked me to play that "popping cannons" song. It took me a few minutes to figure out he meant "Pachelbel's Canon."

As gently as I could, I took Alexander aside and asked him a question. "Alexander, can you explain something to me? Every time we make pictures or tell stories or pick out books, your choices always focus on war. I'm not saying that you are doing anything wrong. I just want to understand. Can you tell me why?"

Alexander was quiet. Then he looked me right in the eye, very seriously, and said, "It's because boys are boys and girls are girls."

Out of the mouth of babes! I did not understand—because boys and girls *are* different. Not better, not worse—just not the same. Of course, the world is filled with millions of gradations: women who have a more strongly developed "masculine side" and men who abhor war and violence. And while we embrace these many gradations, examining traditional roles can reveal some helpful insights.

In Amish families, men and women have different roles. Not better, not worse—just not the same. Within their spheres, both sexes are accorded great responsibility and great authority. In our age we are accustomed to looking at this with skepticism, if not derision, because of the negative connotations we have with defined gender roles—it looks to us like putting people, male or female, in a box. So what is the advantage to the Amish way of clearly defining the roles? Knowing what your role is, learning from a young age how to fill that role competently, and not having expectations turned around 180 degrees at some later date avoids much confusion, anxiety, and confrontation.

I am not saying that we need to revoke the right to vote or that women should be seen and not heard. What I am saying are the simple facts, nothing new: children do best when they have a healthy relationship modeled by both a father and a mother; having two parents working a combined eighty or more hours a week outside the home is not good for personal or family health; and divorce is costly, with single moms and children often bearing the brunt.

Recently, I participated in two gatherings that examined twenty-first-century Christian women's roles. The first panel included four women who were trying to juggle full-time careers, young children, struggling marriages, and church commitments. This panel was followed by four women who had temporarily put amazing careers on hold to care for young children and support husbands with high-visibility roles in the church. I was asked to speak on a third panel—women who worked in ministry alongside their husbands.

Later that night, I asked Matthew for his impressions. His take was exactly the same as mine—the women trying to do it all at once were stressed out. The women who saw life as a long journey, viewing each season as a blessing rather than a trial to be endured, seemed much happier. And the (older) women who also had the privilege of working alongside their husbands, appreciating the strengths they each brought to the table, seemed truly content. While most couples may not be able to serve together professionally, working in tandem at least in some capacity rather than at random with no shared plan seems a goal worth aspiring to.

The following weekend, I was asked to help lead a retreat for college women. This time, nine women in the community were asked to talk about their journeys. Most of the women were in their thirties or forties. One was single, one was divorced, one was married without kids, and one had struggled with infertility and subsequently adopted children. All of us shared a love for Christ and a strong desire to abide in God's will.

Since I spoke last—and was the eldest—I used my time to summarize what I had heard from the other panelists. Through the stories of their lives, each was trying to help this young college audience avoid some of the pitfalls she had encountered. Here are some of the recurring themes they shared:

1. God's plans may be very different from yours.
2. Doors that close are just as valuable as doors that open.
3. In order to hear God's call, you need to be still and listen.
4. You will most likely end up miserable if you try to do everything, all at the same time.
5. God doesn't waste anything.
6. Most women today lead long lives, with many seasons.
7. Part-time work can provide a healthy balance, especially for many women with small children.
8. The world's view of success has nothing to do with God's definition of success.
9. Attitude is everything: if you view supporting your children and husband as an honor, it can be a source of tremendous joy.
10. What you do is far less important than who you are.

These seem to be themes that most women can relate to, regardless of life situation. While I don't believe that the Amish hold the only answers, I do believe that their example can help us ask the right questions. Your choices regarding gender roles may differ from those of your friends and will likely change as life circumstances change. The important point is to keep seeking wisdom—from Scripture, from wise mentors, and from an ever-growing relationship with God.

Give kids chores

Many parents today hesitate to give chores. Because both parents often work—or the kids are being raised by single parents—they feel guilty about asking their kids to wash dishes, fold laundry, or sweep the floor. They have no clear standards for chores and do not enforce consequences. As a result, many parents grow resentful and begin to feel like their children's "slaves."

The Amish, on the other hand, follow the advice of Proverbs 22:6—"Direct your children onto the right path, and when they are older, they will not leave it." Chores are an indispensable aid in helping our children become good spouses, parents, and servants of God. Most Amish teach their children to work in the home and in the garden by the time they are waist high. Everyone is a citizen of the family and each person plays a meaningful role.

Our kids had chores, though my expectations—compared to those of the Amish—were low. They made their beds, cleaned their rooms, and dusted and vacuumed the house, but I definitely hesitated to ask them to do certain jobs, such as scrub toilets, because I did not want to deal with sulking. It was easier to do these things myself. And I did not correct enough; if they missed dusting a lampshade or the base molding, I usually let it pass. In exchanging temporary peace for long-term gain, I did not heed the advice of Hebrews 12:11: "No discipline is enjoyable while it is happening—it's painful! But afterward there will be a peaceful harvest of right living for those who are trained in this way."

In Amish households, helping children grow into competent, unselfish, responsible adults is viewed as a primary responsibility of parenting. The kids learn real skills and reach adulthood well equipped to run their own households and businesses. Modeling Christian maturity is what family life is all about. Scripture is filled with wisdom about raising healthy children, but the passages I find most inspiring are those that compare God's role as our Father with our role as earthly parents. When I feel I am getting off track, Hebrews 12:5-6 is especially helpful:

> My child, don't make light of the LORD's discipline,
>   and don't give up when he corrects you.
> For the LORD disciplines those he loves,
>   and he punishes each one he accepts as his child.

Taking the time to instruct our children—even when we are tired and distracted—is one of the greatest signs of love we can offer.

One of the couples that Matthew and I consider mentors is the pastor of a ten-thousand-member congregation and his wife. While we admire their ability to work together and the beautiful ministry they have built, what we respect most are their parenting skills. Their three grown sons are working for the Kingdom—one as a physician, one as the pastor of a large and vibrant church, and one as a business manager and a church builder, literally. By working along-side their children, this couple has passed along the skills of preaching, healing, and creating—in the image of both their earthly fathers and their heavenly one. I don't think it is an accident that all three of these sons and their families have chosen to live near my friends, so that as grand-parents they can continue to invest in the next generation of servant-leaders.

Like these friends—and the Amish—Matthew and I are committed to passing along skills to the next generation. Though your children may not follow in your vocational footsteps, the time you invest in instruction and loving dis-cipline is certain to have positive ripple effects for decades to come.

Keep the Sabbath

Traditional Amish communities gather for the Sabbath every other Sunday. It is an all-day affair: four hours of worship, Communion, an abundant potluck meal, and time for con-versation and socializing. Families either walk or arrive in buggies. The host family rotates throughout the community. Getting ready for the Sabbath requires the cooperation of everyone in the family.

Early on, Clark and Emma became the biggest defend-ers of our family Sabbath. We cleaned the house together on Saturday. They got their homework done by Saturday evening. On Sunday we walked to a church a few houses down, and then we "put it in park" the rest of the day. We chose not to go to stores or text or e-mail. We read. We took God-ordained naps. We went on walks.

Sabbath keeping is also a central part of my Christian testimony. Raised in a Jewish home, I had always believed in God, but it was not until about a year *after* we started keeping the Sabbath that I came to know Jesus.

One of my favorite Sabbath traditions was to take a hike up a small mountain near our home. I used the time to talk with God and turn over the successes and failures of my week to him. One Sunday afternoon, I started on my walk later than usual. The view from the top of this mountain is surprisingly vast—about forty miles up and down the river valley, a pastoral landscape of dairy farms and white-steepled churches. Seeing the face of God in his creation never failed to calm me.

On this particular Sunday, by the time I came down the mountain it was getting dark and had started to drizzle. Halfway home, I had my "road to Damascus" encounter. Though it did not knock me to the ground or blind me, it was just as transformational. Quite literally, I met a living, breathing Jesus traveling alongside me. As we walked together, he said he would never leave me. And he never has.

While I cannot promise you a Paul-like experience, I can assure you that honoring the Sabbath will change your family in unexpected and positive ways. Jesus told us that humanity was not meant to save the Sabbath; rather, the Sabbath is meant to save humanity. In the midst of the Civil War,

President Lincoln said, "As we keep or break the Sabbath day, we nobly save or meanly lose the last and the best hope by which mankind arises." The Sabbath, as the Amish well know, is also meant to save the family, offering the time and space needed for keeping relationships healthy and intact.

In our technology driven, 24/7 world, families need the Sabbath more than ever. God's rhythm is life giving. Sabbath is a time to refill the well. It is a gift that you and your family are invited to open fifty-two times a year. It is the highlight of the week and will change your family's attitude and interactions during the other six days. Keeping the Sabbath saved our family—in more than one sense of the word—and it can save yours, too.

Let's Sum It Up

Broken families have become the norm in modern society, but an anomaly in Amish communities. What makes Amish families different? Here are a few key factors:

- They live near each other.
- They share meals.
- They respect gender roles.
- They expect children to be citizens of the family.
- They honor the fourth commandment.

What these behaviors have in common are clear expectations and lifelong commitment. Families do not break up, because their first allegiance is to God, not self. Children are not idols to be worshiped. Husbands and wives are not disposable. The (top) Ten Commandments are not optional. Harmony takes precedence over self-interest.

Such harmony can often best be seen when our parenting years are ending and we discover that our children are people we enjoy hanging out with as adults. Let me close with one last vignette of our family. On a beautiful September morning, while I was finishing this chapter, I heard a knock at the door. It was Clark and Val. They were out on a walk and wanted to know if Matthew and I could join them. Matthew was having breakfast with a colleague at Magee's, the neighborhood bakery, so we walked there to see if their meeting was wrapping up. We spotted three of Clark's church friends also having breakfast, and they told us that Matthew had left five minutes ago. We caught up with him on the street, and he joined us, first stopping back at our house so he could change his shoes and I could give Val some fresh goat cheese made by a neighbor. After walking and talking for nearly an hour, I returned—infinitely refreshed—to my writing.

The Amish have a saying: "A happy marriage is a long conversation that always seems too short." And, of course, happy marriages tend to make for happy families. May all your gatherings with family be part of a long conversation, full of joy, harmony, and faith in an all-powerful Father who loves every one of his children.

CHAPTER 10

FAITH

Faith life and way of life are inseparable.

THE AMISH ARE KNOWN for their wise proverbs, but perhaps my favorite consists of just five words: "More is caught than taught." While this saying applies to many areas of life, it is absolutely central to Amish faith. For the Amish, faith is not relegated to an hour on Sundays and then put to the side the rest of the week. Rather, faith is at the center of every action, every day. The Amish, a people of few words, express their faith through example rather than exegesis—by walking the talk rather than only talking the walk.

The Most Powerful Sermon Is the One We Live

When I think of someone who models faith in all aspects of life, Margaret comes immediately to mind. From a very young age, Margaret knew that she wanted to be a doctor and serve others.

Originally, she planned to serve as a medical missionary in Africa, but while attending a Christian medical student gathering she heard a doctor speak about an urban clinic he helped start in an economically challenged neighborhood. Though he earned only $25,000 per year, the same as the typical medical resident, he was able to provide care to everyone, regardless of their ability to pay. The focus of the clinic was on preventive medicine and relationship building. Because faith, not finances, was at the center of Margaret's calling, upon graduation she joined a similar clinic in the poorer section of her city. Margaret has continued to serve that community for nearly three decades.

Margaret's husband is also a physician, raised in Mennonite farm country. Very soon after they each went into practice, it became clear that Margaret and her husband would have more money than they *needed* to live. Instead of ramping up their lifestyle, they looked for ways to live simply and steward their surplus wisely.

One of the first decisions was to purchase a home and several adjoining lots in the less gentrified part of town. They wanted enough land to start a garden and grow some of their own food. In addition to raising four children—including an adopted son—on this urban homestead, Margaret and her husband have invited students, family, and friends to live with them. Some of these visitors have stayed for months; others, years. This hospitality has allowed young people to complete their educations—providing a haven in transitional seasons of life.

Margaret and her husband also wanted to use some of their surplus to stay connected to the land and help family members continue in the farming tradition. When the opportunity arose to purchase property next to her mother-in-law's farm, they bought the land. This land is farmed by Margaret's brother-in-law.

Later in their marriage, Margaret and her husband were asked to speak to a Christian group of medical students about finances. They did something few of us would be brave enough to do: they tallied up all they had earned in the last few years, all they had spent, all they had saved, and all they had given away, and then shared this chart with the students. While most medical students are living on loans, as physicians they will be stewards of significant salaries. Margaret wanted to help these Christian students make good choices about their future lifestyles. The pie chart of Margaret's family finances provided one model of a faith-centered life. As Jesus says, "No one can serve two masters. For you will hate one and love the other; you will be devoted to one and despise the other. You cannot serve both God and money" (Matthew 6:24).

Throughout their three decades of marriage, church has remained a central part of their shared faith life. The main Mennonite church in their city is relatively large and located quite a distance from their home. So Margaret and her husband helped start a smaller sister church closer to their neighborhood, where they continue to attend. The children made friends in the youth group, and Margaret grows her faith through a weekly women's Bible study.

In many ways, the life of Margaret's family sums up much of what we have talked about through this book. Their vocation, home, finances, simple way of living, sense of place, hospitality, and commitment to community and family all reflect a desire to walk in the light of Jesus. Faith is not something that happens once a week in the church pew; it is the totality of how they choose to live. For Margaret and her husband, faith life and way of life are one.

The Almost Amish Way: Faith and Life Are Inseparable

While I respect many things about the Amish, what I admire most is how faith permeates every area of life. Religious beliefs shape the major rites of passage—birth, baptism, Communion, marriage, and death. This is because, for the Amish, the German Bible is the center of faith life. They focus on applying the teachings of Jesus on a daily basis, emphasizing the Gospel of Matthew, especially the Sermon on the Mount (Matthew 5–7).

In addition to the Bible, several other important texts shape Amish beliefs, including the *Martyrs Mirror*, the *Ausbund*, and the Dordrecht Confession of Faith.

Because of their persecution in Europe, the Amish have a history of martyrs for the faith. The 1,100-page *Martyrs Mirror* records these religious persecution and martyr stories that continue to influence Amish values today.

The hymns of the *Ausbund*, many of which were written by imprisoned Anabaptists in the sixteenth century, is the primary songbook used in Amish worship services. Because it does not include musical notations, chants are passed along orally from generation to generation.

The Dordrecht Confession of Faith includes eighteen articles of Christian faith, written by the Dutch Anabaptists in 1632. Candidates for baptism promise to adhere to these articles.

In general, however, the Amish are more concerned with living their beliefs than teaching formal theological doctrine. This becomes clear when we take a look at how they observe the common rituals and major milestones of life.

View each child as a gift, not a god

The attitude toward children begins before birth, with Amish mothers taking pregnancy in stride. Instead of reading self-help books filled with the latest advice for giving birth "your way," expectant moms learn from experience. Most come from families where birth and childrearing are regular parts of life. They have helped their moms with younger siblings or helped older siblings with nieces and nephews. The focus is not on the mother having the perfect birth experience but on gratitude to God for the gift of new life.

The Amish don't give baby showers—having lots of baby paraphernalia is not in keeping with the Amish value of simplicity—nor do moms spend months fussing over nursery decorations and baby outfits. Baby clothes are shared among families, and toys are handed down from generation to generation.

While births can occur in the hospital, most take place at home with a midwife. If complications are suspected, a doctor is often brought in and the couple may barter for the doctor's bill, in part or whole.

In our mainstream world, we don't have to eliminate gifts for newborns—even the Amish make baby quilts. Nor must we eschew modern medicine—even Amish women welcome medical help in complicated births. Yet in our culture of consumption, a baby can sometimes be treated as an idol made in our own image—more as an entitlement than a gift on loan from God.

In many American families, babies become the center of attention. In Amish society, the spotlight remains on God. Babies are loved but not idolized.

Just as God loves us, we are to love our children. God loves us without ever worshiping us. We can do the same.

Keep the rituals of faith: communion and worship

Semiannual Communion and the every-other-week worship services are the central religious rituals in Amish life. These rituals mirror key values of Amish faith—simplicity, humility, community, and submission to God's will.

Communion services, held in the fall and spring each year, emphasize self-examination and spiritual rejuvenation. Prior to the Communion service, members confess their sins and reaffirm their commitment to the Ordnung. Only when the congregation is "at peace"—when all members are in harmony—can Communion be held. The semiannual service includes preaching, a light meal, the commemoration of Christ's death with bread and wine, and pairs of members washing each other's feet as the congregation sings. At the end of the service, members offer alms—the only time a collection is taken during Amish services.

Because the Amish do not have church buildings, they rotate meeting every other Sunday in the home of one of their district members. Each household hosts about once per year. On "off Sundays," families often read the Bible together or visit services in a nearby district.

Church services reflect the simplicity of Amish life. There are no robes, pulpits, altars, candles, organs, stained glass windows, or choirs—no PowerPoint talks or praise bands. Young children sit with their parents throughout the service, and older youth sit in another section, boys on one side, girls on the other.

Slow, unison singing in German, without instruments, is a central part of community worship. In many traditional districts, church leaders decide who will preach that day while the congregation sings the opening hymn. The person selected preaches without any notes, often in Pennsylvania Dutch dialect. The service includes two sermons: a thirty-minute opening sermon and an hour or longer main sermon. In addition, the deacon reads a passage from Scripture. The community kneels while reciting two prayers, one read from a prayer book and the other silent.

The specific ways you celebrate these rituals of faith most likely will differ from the Amish. Yet no matter how often or in what manner you practice them, Communion and worship services play a central role in the faith life of Christians throughout the world. The origin of both "community" and "Communion" comes from the Latin *munus*, which refers to gift, and *cum*, which means together. Practicing these rituals is one important way we can all honor the gift of coming together while keeping our faith life vibrant.

Celebrate baptism as a community

As we discussed earlier, baptism is the most important decision in a young Amish person's life. Most youth take their baptismal vow between the ages of eighteen and twenty-two. The baptismal vow is a lifelong commitment to follow the ways of Jesus and uphold the Ordnung ("order") of the church. While most Amish youth do choose baptism, church membership is voluntary; thus, the baptismal ceremony is both a serious decision and a time for celebration.

Outside the Amish community, baptismal practices vary greatly. Some denominations practice infant baptism, others adult baptism, but the central goal is the same: a lifelong commitment to serving God. Whether the person is being dunked, immersed, or sprinkled, baptism is a beautiful ceremony that always brings tears to my eyes and inspires me to recommit my life to God.

My own baptism was a transformational event for our

entire family. Because Clark, Emma, and I came to know Christ around the same time, we chose to be baptized together. I will never forget kneeling beside my children, feeling the unity we now shared not only with each other but with the family of believers throughout time. It was a multi-handkerchief day for the family, Matthew and me most of all.

One way we can celebrate baptism is to view it as a symbol that requires reaffirmation every waking moment of our lives. In other words, while the ceremony of baptism is a personal commitment to God, celebrating it as a community can be a gift to every witness present, a reminder of how we must continually die to the old ways and be reborn in the light of Christ.

Focus on the marriage, not the wedding

The average wedding in the United States costs more than $26,000; the Amish wedding, by comparison, reflects the values of simplicity, humility, and community. Rather than worrying about bridesmaids' dresses and videographers, the Amish place their emphasis on the sacred bond of marriage. As Jesus says, "'This explains why a man leaves his father and mother and is joined to his wife, and the two are united into one.' Since they are no longer two but one, let no one split apart what God has joined together" (Matthew 19:5-6).

Weddings are joyous but not extravagant. There are no "save the date" refrigerator magnets, tuxedo rentals, limos, or disposable cameras. Brides do not hire wedding planners, and mothers (and fathers) of the couple remain quietly in the background. God, rather than the band leader, stays front and center throughout the celebrations.

The Amish wedding emphasizes sacred commitments made before God and the church district. It is the ceremony that announces a new position in the community and a new relationship as man and wife. Despite (or perhaps in part because of) these simpler weddings, Amish divorce rates are less than one percent—nearly fifty times less than the divorce rate of both Christian and non-Christian marriages in America.

Because many Amish communities remain agriculturally oriented, Amish marriages usually take place from late October through December, after the fall harvest. Tuesdays and Thursdays are the traditional days for weddings. Parents do not select who their children will marry, but they must give their approval. The deacon often acts as the formal go-between for the families.

After the fall Communion ceremony, couples planning to marry are "published" or announced in front of the congregation during the Sunday church service. The bride's parents, however, usually have already begun preparations: one sign of an upcoming marriage is the early summer planting of hundreds of stalks of celery, which are put in jars for table decorations at the wedding and served as a vegetable with the meal.

The marriage service, held in the home of the bride's parents, is similar to the regular Sunday service. Sermons and Bible passages emphasize the relationship between man and wife and the lifelong commitment of marriage.

Because divorce is not considered an option, marriage vows are taken especially seriously. The couple pledges to remain together until death, being loyal and caring for each other throughout adversity, affliction, and illness. The ceremony ends with the minister taking the couple's hands and telling them to "Go forth in the Lord's name." From that day forward, the couple is expected to keep God at the center of the marriage.

After the service, a wedding celebration is held. The traditional meal includes a "roast"—chicken with stuffing, mashed potatoes, coleslaw, applesauce, and creamed celery. Pies, doughnuts, fruit, pudding, and several wedding cakes are often eaten later in the day. It can take several seatings to feed all the guests, using the benches from the wedding service to form tables.

In the afternoon, the young people sing hymns, followed by an evening meal for those who have stayed, and one last hymn sing, with the "faster hymns" prevailing.

The couple spends the wedding night at the bride's home, then helps clean up from the celebration. For the next few months, the newlyweds visit relatives on the weekends, often receiving practical wedding gifts on their visits. By spring, the couple usually is ready to set up their own home.

The Amish have a saying: "Marriage may be made in heaven, but man is responsible for the upkeep." Yes, the wedding is a time for joyous celebration, but the marriage is what matters. To help marriages stay centered on God, the Amish offer a clever memory tool: "**JOY** means Jesus first, Yourself last, and Others in between." That's sound advice every married couple—in fact, every person—would be wise to heed. What a better world it would be if all marriages centered on commitment rather than convenience, on giving rather than receiving, and on God rather than self!

Care for others in times of mourning

Almost every wedding ceremony includes some version of "till death do us part"—a reminder, even in the midst of great hope and joy, of the final major milestone in each of our lives.

I once heard a pastor talk about the saddest funeral at which he ever officiated. When he introduced his subject, I thought that it would involve the terminal illness of a young child or perhaps a father losing his family in a drunk-driving accident. But this death was even more sobering. An elderly man had contacted the pastor, giving explicit instructions for his funeral and paying for the service in advance. When the man died, no one came to the funeral. Feeling obliged to keep his word, the pastor preached the eulogy to rows of empty chairs.

It is difficult to imagine a more dismal funeral, isn't it? Yet for the Amish, it would be impossible. It is a scene that simply cannot happen within their community. With everyone connected to one another, no one dies alone.

Perhaps more than any other passage of life, death brings out the core Amish values of community, simplicity, and humility. While funeral rituals vary somewhat from district to district, it is accepted practice for neighbors to take on household, farm, and work chores for the immediate family.

Friends and relatives also assume responsibility for funeral preparations—making food, setting up benches, and accommodating horses and carriages.

Because funeral rituals are simple, families are not burdened with making expensive or complicated decisions. The body is dressed in white and laid out in an unadorned, hardwood coffin. Friends and relatives visit the family for two days prior to the funeral. Community members dig the grave by hand. Several hundred guests typically attend the funeral, during which the minister reads Scripture, offers prayers, and preaches a sermon.

A large black carriage pulled by horses leads a procession of carriages to the burial ground. At the simple graveside service, pallbearers lower the coffin and shovel soil into the grave as the bishop reads a hymn.

Humility is shown by the smallness of the gravestone—equal in size to every other gravestone in the cemetery. The Amish are a community of equals in death as in life. After the graveside service, family and close friends return home and share a meal.

"Ashes to ashes, dust to dust" is often quoted at funeral services. The point of this phrase is not to make us believe that life is meaningless; rather, it is to remind us that belief is what gives life meaning.

As with all other Amish rituals, the simplicity and humility of the Amish funeral keep the focus where it belongs—on the Creator who groans when a single sparrow falls from the sky. The comfort and aid the Amish give each other surrounding times of death are but reflections of the comfort and aid that God offers each of us throughout our lives.

While your funeral traditions may be very different from those of the Amish, death almost always offers opportunities to be of service to others. Making meals, offering rides and accommodations to visiting relatives, and performing simple chores are ways we can express our love and concern for the living. Sending a note that includes a specific fond memory of the deceased—perhaps one that the family never heard before—can be a great comfort.

Fifteen years ago, my brother drowned in front of my children during a family reunion. One of my friends back home realized that I had only vacation clothes with me, so she went through my closet and sent appropriate apparel that I could wear to the funeral and throughout the week of mourning. While clothes were the last thing on my mind at the time, I will never forget this thoughtful act.

For many, the ministry of presence is of greatest value. Listening while family members retell favorite stories can be a first step toward healing. Praying for the mourners and helping them turn to God for solace can increase the faith of all.

The Fruit of Amish Traditions: Forgiveness and Peace

> Instead, be kind to each other, tenderhearted,
> forgiving one another, just as God through Christ
> has forgiven you.
> EPHESIANS 4:32

You have heard the law that says "love your neighbor"
and hate your enemy. But I say, love your enemies!
Pray for those who persecute you! In that way,
you will be acting as true children of your Father
in heaven.

MATTHEW 5:43-45

The traditions surrounding birth, Communion, worship,
baptism, marriage, and death reinforce Amish values. These
values bear fruit in daily life, particularly through the practices the Amish are best known for—forgiveness and peace.

The most public example of Amish forgiveness took place
after the schoolhouse shooting in Pennsylvania, which we
discussed in chapter 8. Amish elders immediately visited the
widow of the shooter, offering comfort and assistance to the
family and condolences to his grieving parents. This Amish
example sent a powerful message throughout the world: forgiveness is unconditional. Jesus died on the cross to atone for
our sins, not because of what we did but because of who he is.

The true test of any value system is how we act under
duress. Forgiveness, like anything else we value, must be
practiced on a regular basis. If we do not forgive the small
infractions—the cranky response of a tired spouse, the tool a
neighbor forgets to return, the missed appointment with an
overworked friend—how can we forgive the bigger wrongs?

Forgiveness is like the muscle mass of our heart; it must be
exercised regularly in order to function well. Just as walking a
couple of miles a day keeps our hearts healthy, forgiving a few

annoyances and disappointments each day keeps our souls in good shape. The effect of daily exercise is cumulative. If the sidewalks are icy and we miss a few days of walking, no harm done. If we occasionally respond defensively to a provocative remark, the relationship will heal.

Big acts of forgiveness, as in the schoolhouse shooting, do not occur in isolation. They come out of a lifetime of practice, based on a rule book—the Bible—that is eternal. The Author's expectations for us are clearly laid out: "Since God chose you to be the holy people he loves, you must clothe yourselves with tenderhearted mercy, kindness, humility, gentleness, and patience. Make allowance for each other's faults, and forgive anyone who offends you. Remember, the Lord forgave you, so you must forgive others" (Colossians 3:12-13).

When we repent, God forgives. Any crime, any confession is immediately and unconditionally forgiven. We should do likewise.

This forgiveness does not sanction the offense or grant license to repeat it. Forgiveness, freely given, offers something even better: it grows our soul.

Make peace wherever you go

Forgiveness is the leavening agent of peace. A couple of teaspoons can help a whole bowl of dough rise. We see this in our families, in our communities, in our nations, and in our world. Grudges held too tightly can spoil the entire batch.

When we invite people for a meal, I almost always serve homemade bread. Bread is often referred to as the "staff of life," an apt description of its restorative power. The smell of bread baking makes entering our home more welcoming. The knowledge that I kneaded that dough makes our guests feel more valued. And the taste of the bread comforts us, especially when that bread is still warm from the oven.

I have included several of my favorite bread recipes in the appendixes, but here's a recipe that feeds our souls.

Peace Bread

Ingredients:
  2 c. unbleached thoughtfulness
  2 c. patience
  1 tsp. empathy
  2 Tbs. melted love
  3 Tbs. sweetness of honey
  1 c. warm milk of kindness
  2 tsp. forgiveness

Instructions:
  Combine kindness, sweetness, and forgiveness in a small bowl until frothy. Mix with the remaining ingredients and gently knead. Place dough in a greased bowl, cover, and allow to rise in a warm place until double in size. Remove dough and knead again. If dough feels stiff, add up to a quarter cup of compassion. Form into desired shape for second rising. Bake in oven until golden. Serve warm.

My soft spot for corny illustrations aside, this metaphor takes on deeper significance when we consider the sacrament—the sacred act—of Communion. When we take Communion, we eat a piece of bread, symbolic of the body of Christ. The Eucharist act unifies the greater body of Christ. As the apostle Paul so eloquently explains in a letter to the Corinthians, each of us within the body of Christ can serve an important role.

In another famous epistle, Paul also makes clear the need for us to practice peace: "Do all that you can to live in peace with everyone" (Romans 12:18). One role of the Amish community is to remind us, through example, how to live in peace with one another. Like forgiveness, the skills for peaceful living grow stronger with practice. Every time we choose to stay calm in traffic, to not shout at a telephone solicitor, or to encourage the losing team is a victory for peace.

A professor at a Christian college shared this life-changing story of peace: He has three sons, all gifted athletes who played sports throughout their school years. This father wanted to be supportive of his sons and attended most of their games. One Saturday afternoon, he found himself in the bleachers screaming loudly at the opposing team. The words coming out of his mouth were not exactly G-rated, and his tone was decidedly angry. He didn't need a mirror to know that his face was red up to the roots of his flattop—jaw hardened and eyes nearly squinted shut in anger.

In one of those rare flashes of self-awareness, however, God held up a mirror. For a brief moment, this father glimpsed how he must look and sound to parents of the student athletes on the opposing team. More important, he saw how his behavior must appear to God—distorted with rage, over what? A basketball game!

That moment of insight changed this man forever. Does he ever feel himself growing angry? Of course. But the mirror that God held up revealed an image he never wants to repeat. His example has taught me that peaceful behaviors *can* be learned; all it takes is the will to change, the endurance to practice, and the faith that, with God's help, transformation will happen.

Let's Sum It Up

Jesus says his followers are in the world but not of it (see John 17:15-16). How do we find the strength and wisdom for such a life? Through faith, and faith grows with practice.

Incorporating Amish values into daily rituals and rites of passage reminds us how faith can permeate every area of our lives. We are God's children not just on Sundays, but every day of the week. Whether we are at work, at home, in the car, or on the soccer field, we are to act with compassion and love. What we do and say does matter, not only to our friends and family, but to our Father. God sees not only our actions but our motivations—our heart writ large, as clear as a neon billboard on Times Square.

Where we seek spiritual guidance also matters. The Bible warns of a time when people "will follow their own desires and will look for teachers who will tell them whatever their itching ears want to hear" (2 Timothy 4:3). Throughout this book, we have used the Amish example to counter such impulses, reminding us time and again, as C. S. Lewis advises in *Mere Christianity*, that "Going back can sometimes be the quickest way forward."

While the Almost Amish guidance throughout this book may not always sound hip or politically correct, it is thoroughly scriptural and relevant. On our Almost Amish journey, each of us can take small steps toward a life where,

- Homes are simple, uncluttered, and clean; the outside reflects the inside.
- Technology serves as a tool and does not rule as a master.
- Saving more and spending less bring financial peace.
- Spending time in God's creation reveals the face of God.
- Small and local leads to saner lives.
- Service to others reduces loneliness and isolation.
- The only true security comes from God.
- Knowing neighbors and supporting local businesses build community.
- Family ties are lifelong; they change but never cease.
- Faith life and way of life are inseparable.

As we give and receive forgiveness, our lives become more peaceful. As we slow down, we are able to hear God's voice. When we simplify, we have more to give to others. And when we set boundaries, our lives become more sustainable, calm, and joyful.

The Almost Amish life is a conscious life. Though the choices we make may vary, it is a journey that we can take together—and above all, with God. Will there be false starts throughout our life with Christ? Of course! The busyness of modern life has a way of thwarting even the best of intentions. Yet each time we seek out an Almost Amish path, we move one step nearer to the Kingdom of God. Every time we choose the Almost Amish way, we come one breath closer to a slower, simpler, more sustainable life.

At one time or another, many of us have been amazed when God puts *exactly* the right Scripture before us, at precisely the moment we need it. In my regular Bible reading, I have been studying the teachings of Jeremiah.

> This is what the Lord says:
> "Stop at the crossroads and look around.
> Ask for the old, godly way, and walk in it.
> Travel its path, and you will find rest for your souls."
> JEREMIAH 6:16

This wisdom bears repeating: *Stop at the crossroads. Ask for the old, godly way. Travel its path, and you will find rest for your souls.* I wish I could say that from the start of this book I had planned to use this amazingly spot-on passage in the closing paragraphs, but the truth is even better: God's perfect timing saved the best for last!

Thanks to that man in the back of the room with the booming voice, I now have an answer to his question, "What are you, Amish or something?"

"Not Amish—*Almost* Amish!"

My prayer is that wherever you are along the Almost Amish path, you have the will, passion, and energy to make one change—however small—this very day. My prayer is that you gain joy in drawing closer to God and lean on him for the strength needed to carry through. My prayer is that you find the peace that passes all understanding as you continue along the Almost Amish journey. May God bless you with his love and protection every step of the way!

Almost Amish Recipes

SERVING SOUP, salad, and bread is one of the easiest (and most flexible) ways to feed family and friends. Most soups taste even better the second day, so plan for leftovers. If more people show up than expected, you can always expand the soup with a bit more stock. For a heartier meal, offer grilled chicken or salmon to top the salad. And feel free to modify according to your family's tastes and what's in season—these recipes are very forgiving, a trait that the Amish have in abundance!

BREADS

Homemade bread makes any meal special. I have provided three favorite recipes with traditional instructions. To keep things simple, however, I almost always use a hybrid system: after mixing the ingredients and completing the first rising in my bread maker, I shape the loaves, place them in a warm spot to rise, and then bake the bread in the oven.

Each recipe makes two loaves—one to eat and one to

send home with guests or share with neighbors, *if* there are any leftovers! Be sure to take a stick of butter out of the refrigerator before the second rising, so it will be spreadable by mealtime.

Honey Whole Wheat with Poppy Seeds

This is my signature bread—the one that repeat guests most often request. It's best served warm from the oven with softened butter. If there are leftovers, sprinkle a slice with cinnamon sugar and pop it in the microwave for a few seconds—depending on the time of a day, it makes a healthy dessert or a memorable breakfast treat. Butter and milk can be omitted if you have vegans among you.

> 1½ c. warm water
> 1 Tbs. canola oil or butter
> 3 Tbs. honey
> ⅓ c. dried milk
> ½ tsp. salt
> 2 c. unbleached white flour
> 2 c. whole wheat flour
> ⅓ c. oat bran hot cereal,
>   dry/uncooked (optional)
> 2 Tbs. poppy seeds
> 2 tsp. fast-rising dry yeast

Mix all ingredients. Knead. Cover and allow to rise in a warm place until double. (Or use the "dough only" setting on your bread maker.) Punch down and knead again. If dough feels sticky, add more flour.

Divide dough into halves and shape into two loaves. Place in greased 4x8 bread pans and allow to rise in a warm place until about double. Bake in preheated oven (350° degrees) for 25–30 minutes or until loaves sound hollow when tapped. Remove from pans and, if desired, run a stick of butter quickly over top of bread. Allow to cool slightly before slicing.

For rolls: Shape dough into 1½-inch round balls before second rising. Place two inches apart on baking sheets coated with nonstick spray. Bake 10 minutes at 350° or until done.

For a change of pace: Omit poppy seeds. Knead in ¾ c. dried cranberries before second rising.

Challah (Jewish braided egg bread)

This is the most beautiful bread I make. One Easter, a pastor friend asked me to bake several loaves for Communion. What a joyful way to meditate upon the risen Christ! If you have any leftovers, challah makes unforgettable French toast.

¾ c. warm milk
2 Tbs. butter or canola oil (optional)
3 eggs
1 tsp. salt
4 c. unbleached white flour
¼–½ c. oat bran hot cereal, dry/uncooked (optional)

2 Tbs. sugar

2 tsp. fast-rising dry yeast

Mix all ingredients. Knead. Cover and allow to rise in a warm place until double. (Or use "dough only" setting on your bread maker.) Punch down and knead again. Add more flour, if dough feels sticky, then divide dough into halves.

Divide each half into three equal pieces (six total). Roll each piece into a long rope—try to make the ropes about the same length and thickness. Coat two baking sheets with nonstick spray. Braid three ropes together on each baking sheet. Moisten fingers and seal ends where the three ropes join.

Allow to rise in a warm place, uncovered, until double. Bake at 350° degrees for 12–15 minutes or until the top is golden and the bread sounds hollow when tapped. Do not overcook. If desired, lightly rub top of warm loaves with butter.

Cinnamon Roll

I have absolutely no willpower when it comes to this bread. Fortunately, neither do those around the table, so there are rarely leftovers!

1 c. warm water

1 egg

2 Tbs. canola oil or butter (optional)

1 tsp. salt

3 c. unbleached white flour

⅓ c. oat bran hot cereal,
   dry/uncooked (optional)

3 Tbs. sugar

1 tsp. vanilla extract

2 tsp. active dry yeast

For filling:

2–4 Tbs. soft butter

½ c. sugar mixed with 3 Tbs. cinnamon

Mix all ingredients except filling. Knead. Place in greased bowl, cover, and allow to rise until double. (Or use "dough only" setting on your bread maker.) Divide into halves.

Knead again, adding additional flour if too sticky, then roll out on floured surface into two rectangles, about ¾-inch thick. Spread dough with thin coat of soft butter. Sprinkle dough liberally with cinnamon-sugar mixture. Roll long edge into a log.

Place logs on baking sheets that have been coated with nonstick spray. Allow to rise, uncovered, in warm place until double. Bake in preheated oven (350°) for 12–15 minutes or until bread sounds hollow when tapped. Do not overcook. If desired, lightly rub top of logs with butter and sprinkle with additional cinnamon-sugar mixture. Best if served warm, but finger-lickin' good anytime.

SOUPS

Soup is my go-to meal both for weeknight dinners and for feeding a crowd. These foolproof recipes serve 4–6 (depending on whether you have teenage boys in the household!) but can easily be doubled or tripled. If desired, adapt for (or keep warm in) a slow cooker—so you can prepare earlier in the day and not be frazzled at mealtime.

My Best Mushroom Soup

I have never had this soup turn out less than spectacular. For a special treat, mix in some shiitake or oyster mushrooms with the domestic mushrooms. When we lived in Wilmore, Kentucky, a neighbor grew and sold exotic mushrooms on a small scale and kept me supplied. Talk about local—and fresh!

4 Tbs. butter, divided
1 c. chopped onion
¼ tsp. salt
¾ lb. mushrooms, sliced—use several varieties,
    if available
1 Tbs. minced fresh dill weed, or 1 tsp. dried
2 c. chicken or vegetable broth, divided
1 Tbs. tamari (or soy) sauce
1 Tbs. sweet Hungarian paprika (or regular paprika)
3 Tbs. all-purpose flour
1 c. milk

2 tsp. lemon juice
Salt and freshly ground pepper to taste
For garnish: ½ c. sour cream plus extra dill weed

In a medium saucepan, sauté onion in 2 Tbs. butter until translucent. Sprinkle lightly with salt. Add mushrooms, dill weed, ½ c. broth, tamari sauce, and paprika. Cover saucepan and simmer for 15 minutes.

Heat remaining 2 Tbs. butter in a soup pot. Whisk in flour and cook, stirring, until the mixture bubbles. Add milk and whisk vigorously to blend well. Return to moderate heat and continue to whisk until sauce is thickened and smooth, about 5 minutes.

Stir in the mushroom mixture and remaining broth. Cover pot and simmer for 10 to 15 minutes.

Just before serving, add lemon juice, salt, and pepper to taste. Garnish each bowl with a generous spoonful of sour cream and a sprinkle of extra dill weed.

Creamy Potato Soup

This is my richest soup—always a winner. Best served with a simple salad, as opposites attract!

3 Tbs. butter
1 c. chopped onion
1 tsp. minced garlic
2 large potatoes, well scrubbed and coarsely chopped
1 large carrot, chopped

3 c. chicken or vegetable stock
1 tsp. dried dill weed, or 2 tsp. fresh
4 oz. cream cheese
1½ c. milk
1 c. grated sharp cheddar cheese
Salt and pepper to taste
Optional: chopped fresh parsley or chives for garnish

In soup pot, sauté onion and garlic in butter until the onion is translucent. Add potatoes and carrot and sauté for 5 minutes longer. Add stock and dill weed and simmer until all vegetables are tender.

Puree cream cheese and half of vegetable mixture in blender until smooth. Return to soup pot and stir in milk and grated cheese. Season with salt and pepper. Garnish each bowl with fresh parsley or chives, if available—the green adds a welcome burst of color!

For Fish Chowder: Add ½ c. clam juice along with stock, substitute ⅛ tsp. Old Bay Seasoning for the dill, and substitute 2 c. cooked, cubed fish or 1 c. chopped clams for the cheese.

Curried Lentil Soup

I adapted this soup from a curried lentil recipe my friend (and fabulous cook!) Bethany shared with me. Cheap, easy, filling, and delicious—the perfect food quadrilateral! Adjust the seasoning for your family's palate, but if you are expecting guests, err on the side of mild and provide extra hot sauce at the table. Our family prefers Sriracha sauce (a.k.a "rooster sauce," because of the image on the bottle), which is inexpensive and available at most Asian markets and larger grocery stores. But beware, a tiny dab goes a long way!

1½ c. dried lentils (Brown lentils are okay, but if you
    can find yellow, orange, or green lentils, they are
    well worth the extra expense.)
1 bay leaf
1 tsp. sea salt
5 c. chicken or vegetable broth
¼ c. butter
1 large onion, chopped
1 clove garlic, minced
¼ tsp. sea salt
1–2 tsp. curry powder (to taste)
2 Tbs. lemon juice
3 c. cooked rice (brown or white), optional
Optional garnishes: hot sauce, grated cheese, and
    sour cream or plain yogurt

Combine first four ingredients and bring to a boil, then simmer for 20 minutes. Remove bay leaf.

While the lentils cook, sauté onion and garlic in butter until translucent, about 10 minutes. Sprinkle with the ¼ tsp. sea salt and add the curry powder. Cook 3 minutes longer. Mix onion mixture and lemon juice into lentils.

For a more filling meal, serve the lentil soup over hot rice.

Provide hot sauce, grated cheese, and sour cream or plain yogurt, to add as desired.

Wedding Soup (Italian Meatball Soup with Orzo)

This is one of Matthew's favorite soups and incredibly easy to make! I prepare this for guests only if I know we don't have any vegetarians at the table—it is a very hearty soup and especially filling when extra broth is sopped up with fresh bread.

2 Tbs. butter
¾ c. diced onion
1 c. diced carrots
5 c. chicken broth
1 beef bouillon cube
1 c. dried orzo
30 cooked meatballs, freshly made or frozen
Total of 1 tsp. dried or 2 tsp. fresh Italian herbs
    (such as basil, oregano, and parsley)
Salt and pepper to taste
½ c. diced spinach or other fresh greens
Optional: grated Parmesan cheese

In a soup pot, sauté onion and carrots in butter until soft, about 10 minutes. Add broth and bouillon cube and continue cooking 10 minutes more.

Meanwhile, in a separate pot, cook orzo according to package directions until firm, about 6 minutes. When onion and carrots are tender, add meatballs, Italian herbs, and cooked, drained orzo. Season with salt and pepper to taste.

Stir in diced greens and cook for one minute longer. Spoon into bowls and offer optional grated Parmesan cheese at the table.

Note: If you plan to have leftovers, add orzo to each bowl rather than to the soup pot. Orzo expands, so it will soak up all the broth overnight.

Tortellini Soup

This recipe is the holy grail for the gourmet in a hurry—an elegant meal, with almost no mess or hassle! When your family and guests compliment you, just say "thank you" and leave it at that.

4 c. (about 3 pkg.) *fresh* wild mushroom tortellini or ravioli (or substitute another favorite fresh tortellini/ ravioli, found in the refrigerated pasta section of the grocery store)

5 c. chicken or vegetable broth

4 firm plum tomatoes, seeded and chopped

½ c. five-cheese spaghetti sauce (I prefer Bertolli brand.)

Total of 1 tsp. dried or 2 tsp. fresh Italian herbs (such as basil, oregano, and parsley)

Salt and pepper to taste

Optional garnish: shredded Parmesan cheese and additional fresh, chopped herbs

Mix broth, chopped tomatoes, spaghetti sauce, and herbs in soup pot. Bring to vigorous boil. Add tortellini and cook 4–5 minutes until al dente. Add salt and pepper to taste.

Garnish with fresh herbs, if available, and serve with shredded Parmesan cheese.

Note: Pasta will get mushy if kept in soup stock overnight. However, this recipe is so simple you can always make a fresh batch!

Cream of Whatever Soup

Consider this soup your chance to be creative with whatever vegetables are in season. Fresh croutons will make this soup a feast: cube some leftover bread and toast in a hot pan with plenty of oil, minced garlic, and chopped parsley. Float croutons on top of soup just before serving.

3 c. broccoli, asparagus, or other in-season vegetable—
   cooked and drained
3 Tbs. butter
1 tsp. minced garlic
3 Tbs. all-purpose flour
1 c. milk
2 c. chicken or vegetable broth
1½ c. grated Muenster, Swiss, or cheddar cheese
Salt and pepper to taste
1 tsp. dried dill weed or 2 tsp. fresh

Melt butter in soup pot, cook garlic for one minute, then add flour. Stir over medium heat until mixture bubbles. Slowly whisk in milk and broth; cook until sauce thickens, about 10 minutes.

Add grated cheese and stir until melted and smooth. Place cooked vegetable in a blender and add sauce; process to desired consistency. Add salt, pepper, and dill to taste.

If soup is too thick (or you have more mouths to feed), thin with additional milk and/or broth. Serve hot, topped with fresh croutons.

SALADS

Salads in our house are inspired by the season—based on what is plentiful in the garden and farmers' market. Be creative! Besides the usual vegetables, consider these toppings to add substance and color to your salads:

- Sliced strawberries, diced avocado, and goat cheese (chèvre)

- Blueberries and feta cheese

- Dried cranberries, blue cheese, and pecans (Clark's favorite)

- Mandarin oranges and slivered almonds

- Cold (briefly steamed) broccoli and cauliflower florets and shredded Parmesan

- Diced apples (or slightly under-ripe pears), walnuts, and grated extra-sharp cheddar

- Cold steamed asparagus tips and grated Gouda or baby Swiss

- Golden raisins and cashews

- Small cubes of fresh mozzarella and roasted or sun-dried tomatoes

- Drained artichoke hearts (diced), homemade croutons, and shredded Parmesan

- Grilled chicken or salmon. See my favorite marinade below.

Chicken or Salmon Marinade

Mix 1 part canola oil and one part soy sauce. Add salt, pepper, minced garlic, and dried dill to taste. Marinate chicken or salmon for at least 20 minutes, turning once.

Nancy's Honey Mustard Vinaigrette

I nearly always serve salad with homemade dressing. This is my tried-and-true recipe, but feel free to personalize it with different vinegars and flavorings.

½ c. olive oil
⅓ c. balsamic vinegar
1 tsp. Dijon mustard

1 tsp. honey
½ tsp. dried dill weed
Salt and pepper to taste

Place all ingredients in tightly covered jar and shake well.

Additional Resources

INTERESTED IN LEARNING more about the Almost Amish
life? Here are a few recommended resources for further
exploration:

- For practical applications and downloadable tip sheets,
  visit www.blessedearth.org/resources.

- My favorite website for learning more about the Amish
  is http://www.etown.edu/centers/young-center/. This
  link takes you to Elizabethtown College's Young Center
  for Anabaptist and Pietist Studies.

- For an interested layperson, the most thorough book
  for studying this subject is *Amish Society*, by John
  A. Hostetler (The Johns Hopkins University Press).
  Professor Hostetler was the former director of the
  Elizabethtown Young Center.

- If you watch just one movie about the Amish, I recommend *Amish Grace*. It may not have Hollywood

high-budget production value, but the story of forgiveness under the most horrific circumstances is so
compelling that I would list it among the top ten
most-moving films.

- The Mennonite *More-with-Less Cookbook* and *Living
  More with Less* guidebook are much beloved resources
  in many households, including ours. I was blown
  away (and more than a little humbled) when asked
  to write the introduction to the thirtieth anniversary edition. Consider this an unabashed plug for
  my Mennonite (and, as Matthew says, "Mostly
  Mennonite") friends around the globe!

- If you are fortunate enough to have an Amish community near you, plan a fun and educational day trip.
  Or, if you are visiting the mid-Atlantic region, include
  a visit to the epicenter of Amish culture, Lancaster,
  Pennsylvania. Slow down. Visit some local businesses.
  Spend time in the surrounding countryside. Seeing is
  believing, and believing will help you see!

- The best way to embark on any journey is with the
  support of friends. Use the discussion guide that follows in your church's small group or with a circle of
  like-minded neighbors. Wherever you are along the
  Almost Amish journey, encourage one another, and
  know that I am with you in spirit, cheering you along
  every step of the way!

Questions for Further Thought or Discussion

Introduction

1. On page xii Nancy and her husband had a transformational conversation while enjoying God's creation on a starlit night. Describe a time when you felt close to God while out in nature.

2. This conversation eventually led Nancy and her family to significantly simplify their lives. What are some things you could do to reduce your ecological footprint or simplify your life?

3. Which of the Amish principles described on page xxi would you most want to try incorporating into your life? Why?

Chapter 1

1. In what ways can pride be manifested in our homes?

2. Jesus' call to us is to follow him and leave everything behind (p. 6). While we might not be prepared to do this all at once, what could some first steps look like?

3. Nancy says that the Amish way is to buy only what is truly needed (p. 8). What would some of these items be for you? Name some items that you only *think* you need.

4. What are some ways you could "invite all to your table," opening your home to others?

5. How does your home reflect your values?

Chapter 2

1. Nancy writes, "Technology serves as a tool and does not rule as a master" (p. 25). Is this true for you? Why or why not?

2. In what ways can "opting out" (p. 27) affect your life?

3. Has technology supplanted God in any sense in your heart and your affections? Explain.

4. Of the five tips Nancy gives on pages 33–44 for making conscious choices about technology (turn off your cell phone, limit/eliminate TV, cut back on computer games, reduce incoming e-mail, and approach social media with caution), which would be hardest for you and/or your family? Why?

Chapter 3

1. How would you answer the questions Nancy poses on pages 50–51? Are you surprised by your responses?

2. In what ways is Reverend Martin Luther King Jr.'s fear that people are becoming more concerned with "making a living than making a life" (p. 55) represented in your workweek? In what ways could you improve on this?

3. If you honestly adhered to the biblical statement "God owns everything" (p. 66), how might your thinking about finances be affected?

Chapter 4

1. In what ways are you showing your appreciation for God's creation? How does your love for creation show in your love for God?

2. Nancy gives six ways to abide in God in his natural world (grow a garden, pack a picnic, pick up trash, plant a tree, work outdoors, and play outdoors). Which do you think would be the hardest and which the easiest to include in your daily life?

3. If you took Nancy's advice and spent more time in nature, in what ways might your relationship with God be affected?

Chapter 5

1. Nancy asks, "What does a holistic approach to simplicity involve?" (p. 94). How would you answer this question?

2. If you were to cut back on the two kinds of stuff that inhibit simplicity (the stuff that fills your house and the stuff that fills your calendars), which would be more difficult?

3. Do you have a network of neighbors? Why or why not?

Chapter 6

1. Nancy writes, "Service is the agent through which we act out our love for God and for one another" (p. 111). How is this evident in your life?

2. In what ways do you see God's service to you? In what ways are you serving God?

3. Is there anything you are withholding from God that you can see is becoming an idol in your life?

4. Are you serving God by giving him your firstfruits? Why or why not?

Chapter 7

1. Are the Amish guidelines for security (tradition, stability, sense of place) missing from your life? In what ways could you incorporate these ideals?

2. Of the three storm stories Nancy describes (pp. 136–137), which do you identify with the most? Explain.

3. What traditions do you have with your family? What traditions could you weave back into your life to build security in your family?

4. In what ways could you reach out to your brothers and sisters in Christ, especially when it might be inconvenient or costly?

Chapter 8

1. How has new technology replaced human contact in your life? In what ways can this be changed?

2. What might be the challenges of buying primarily from local businesses? How can some of these challenges be overcome?

3. Of the ways Nancy provides to have fun building community (pp. 167–168), in which do you think you are most likely to participate?

4. What are some of the potential benefits of taking an active part in your community?

Chapter 9

1. Nancy writes that a common theme in Amish tradition is harmony (p. 177). What are some specific ways you could help increase harmony in your family life?

2. Which of the five Almost Amish actions (stay close geographically, share family meals, respect gender roles, give kids chores, and keep the Sabbath) would be the easiest to add to your family life? Which would be the most difficult? Why?

3. How do you think that keeping the Sabbath might affect the other six days of the week? How might it affect your relationship with God?

Chapter 10

1. Is your faith permeating every aspect of your life as it does for many of the Amish? In what ways could you incorporate your faith on a daily basis?

2. How could you show your love for God through worship?

3. The Amish are best known for practicing forgiveness and peace. Which of these two practices do you wish were stronger in your life?

4. Has God ever held a mirror up to your face? What do you think he was trying to tell you, and what did you see?

5. Name at least three specific changes that you have made or would like to make in your life as a result of reading *Almost Amish*.

Acknowledgments

THE PARABLE of the ten lepers teaches us to give thanks to those who give us life. "Thank you" is a mere shadow of the gratitude I feel for the family and friends who gave life to this book.

Matthew: You are the love of my life. Thanks for more than thirty years of love, friendship, walks, and laughter. You helped me see the Creator and his creation with new eyes. Most of all, thank you for bringing Jesus into my life.

Emma: I can think of no greater peace than having you rest on my shoulder. Thank you for playing Scrabble, baking perfect challah, and reminding me to have fun. You make being green not only easy but beautiful. I will always be your "me-mommy."

Clark: You are the least materialistic and most humble person I know. Thank you for dedicating your life to God and to "healing the people." Being your mother has been one of the greatest privileges of my life.

Valerie: The greatest gift Clark ever gave me was you, our brilliantly beautiful daughter-in-law. Your love for the Lord and your love for my son bring me joy every moment of every day. You are an answer to many prayers, and I love you dearly.

Greg: This book wouldn't have happened without you. Some people have friends. Others have agents. We are blessed to have both in you.

Cara: You are an editing angel—extraordinarily patient, kind, funny, and wise. Thank you for making *Almost Amish* at least a zillion times better. I truly, truly could not have done it without you.

Carol: When you drove down to Kentucky to meet us for the first time, I knew we would be friends for life. Thank you for being my sister in Christ and for putting together the Tyndale dream team. Thank you for believing. It's been a match made in heaven.

The Tyndale Team: To Ron Beers, Lisa Jackson, April Kimura-Anderson in marketing, the incredible designers, the indefatigable copyeditors and proofreaders, the national sales team, and all the other people who made *Almost Amish* possible—thank you for honoring Christ in everything you do and say. It's pure joy to work with you.

Mom and Dad: You give new meaning to "unconditional love." Thank you for more than five decades of warm hugs and shared lives. You are the best cheerleaders a daughter could ask for. I love you both dearly.

Margie and Leslie: "Friends may come and go, but sisters are forever." Thanks for always being there. Richard: I miss you. We all do. Very much.

The Blessed Earth board and our Blessed Earth friends throughout the world: Your love and encouragement sustain us. Thank you for your inspiration and for all you do to care for God's creation. We are grateful.

Diane Ives and the Angel Kendeda: You make dreams come true. Every day, we thank God for you.

The Spicers: You are our second family. Thank you for your counsel, friendship, faith, and generosity. You model what it means to live as Christians, on-call for God and his broken people, 24/7.

Geoff and Sherry: You are my heroes. Thank you for providing care for our souls. You live with and love the least among us, just as Jesus calls us to do.

Linda and Terre: Laughter and tears; prayers and thanksgiving; grief and joy. Our gatherings feed me, physically and spiritually. It would be a lonely journey without you.

To the Amish and Mennonite people: Thank you for continuing to live out the principles of simplicity and sustainability. Thank you for showing me how faith life and way of life are one. Please accept my apologies for any inadvertent errors, and my gratitude for the living example you are.

To all the friends who allowed me to share their stories and the people around the country who invite us into their churches and their lives: This book is for you.

God: Thank you for being who you are—Creator and Sustainer, Artist and Inventor, Gardener, Shepherd, the Rock. Thank you for putting your Son by my side as I walked down the mountain. Thank you for never leaving me. You are the author of my life, my friend, my Savior.

About the Author

NANCY SLEETH and her husband of thirty years, Matthew, are cofounders of Blessed Earth, a faith-based environmental nonprofit. After an environmental and spiritual conversion experience, Nancy and her family radically altered their footprint, giving away half their possessions and reducing their energy use by more than two-thirds. Prior to heeding this environmental calling, Nancy served as communications director for a Fortune 500 company and as an educator and administrator, most recently at Asbury University. She is a graduate of Georgetown University and holds a master's degree in journalism. Nancy and Matthew are the parents of Clark, a medical resident preparing for missionary work, and Emma, the author of *It's Easy Being Green* (Zondervan), which is a call to teens to live sustainable lifestyles. The Sleeths live in Lexington, Kentucky.